Editor
Mary S. Jones, M.A.

Editor in Chief
Karen J. Goldfluss, M.S. Ed.

Cover Artists
Tony Carillo
Brenda DiAntonis

Imaging
James Edward Grace

Publisher

Mary D. Smith, M.S. Ed.

Correlations to the Common Core State Standards can be found at *http://www.teachercreated.com/standards/*.

DAILY WA...

Nonfiction Reading

Grade 3

TCR 5033

M000251493

CORRELATED TO COMMON CORE STANDARDS

Includes:

➤ 150 leveled passages with a variety of interesting topics

➤ Comprehension questions that target reading skills & strategies

➤ Standards & Benchmarks

30 passages & activities in each of these sections:
Interesting Places & Events
Scientifically Speaking
From the Past
Did You Know?
Fascinating People

Ideal for test preparation

Teacher Created Resources

Author

Debra J. Housel, M.S. Ed.

Teacher Created Resources
6421 Industry Way
Westminster, CA 92683
www.teachercreated.com

ISBN: 978-1-4206-5033-4

©2011 Teacher Created Resources
Reprinted, 2013
Made in U.S.A.

Teacher Created Resources

Table of Contents

Table of Contents (cont.)

Introduction

The primary goal of any reading task is comprehension. *Daily Warm-Ups: Nonfiction Reading* uses high-interest, grade-level appropriate nonfiction passages followed by assessment practice to help develop confident readers who can demonstrate their skills on standardized tests. Each passage is a high-interest nonfiction text that fits one of the five topic areas: Interesting Places and Events, Scientifically Speaking, From the Past, Did You Know?, and Fascinating People. Each of these five topic areas has 30 passages, for a total of 150 passages. Each passage, as well as its corresponding multiple-choice assessment questions, is provided on one page.

Comprehension Questions

The questions in *Daily Warm-Ups: Nonfiction Reading* assess all levels of comprehension, from basic recall to critical thinking. The questions are based on fundamental reading skills found in scope-and-sequence charts across the nation:

- recall information
- use prior knowledge
- visualize
- recognize the main idea
- identify supporting details
- understand cause and effect

- sequence in chronological order
- identify synonyms and antonyms
- know grade-level vocabulary
- use context clues to understand new words
- make inferences
- draw conclusions

Readability

The texts have a 3.0–4.0 grade level based on the Flesch-Kincaid Readability Formula. This formula, built into Microsoft Word®, determines readability by calculating the number of words, syllables, and sentences. Multisyllabic words tend to skew the grade level, making it appear higher than it actually is. Refer to the Leveling Chart on page 174 for the approximate grade level for each passage.

In some cases, there are words necessary to a passage that increase its grade level. In those cases, the passage's grade level is followed by an asterisk in the chart. This means that in determining the grade level, the difficult words were factored in, resulting in the increased level shown before the asterisk. Upon the removal of these words, the passage received a grade level within the appropriate range. For example, in the passage, "Alaska, America's Final Frontier," the grade level is 4.6. This is because the word "Alaska" is repeated several times. Once this word is removed, the grade level is within range.

Including Standards and Benchmarks

The passages and comprehension questions throughout this book also correlate with McREL (Mid-Continent Research for Education and Learning) Standards. Known as a "Compendium of Standards and Benchmarks," this resource is well researched. It includes standards and benchmarks that represent a consolidation of national and state standards in several content areas for grades K–12. (See page 6 for the specific McREL Standards and Benchmarks that correspond with this book.) These standards have been aligned to the Common Core State Standards. To view them, please visit *http://www.teachercreated.com/standards/*.

Introduction *(cont.)*

Practice First to Build Familiarity

Initial group practice is essential. Read aloud the first passage in each of the five topic areas and do its related questions with the whole class. Depending upon the needs of your class, you may choose to do the first three passages in each topic area as a whole class. Some teachers like to use five days in a row to model the reading and question-answering process at the start of the year. Model pre-reading the questions, reading the text, highlighting information that refers to the comprehension questions, and eliminating answers that are obviously incorrect. You may also want to model referring back to the text to ensure the answers selected are the best ones.

Student Practice Ideas

With *Daily Warm-Ups: Nonfiction Reading* you can choose to do whole-class or independent practice. For example, you can use the passages and questions for any of the following:

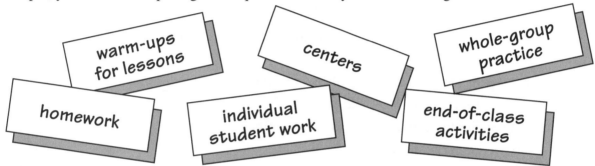

warm-ups for lessons

centers

whole-group practice

homework

individual student work

end-of-class activities

Whichever method you choose for using the book, it's a good idea to practice as a class how to read a passage and respond to the comprehension questions. In this way, you can demonstrate your own thought processes by "thinking aloud" to figure out an answer. Essentially this means that you tell your students your thoughts as they come to you.

Record Keeping

In the sun image at the bottom, right-hand corner of each warm-up page, there is a place for you (or for students) to write the number of questions answered correctly. This will give consistency to scored pages. Use the tracking sheet on page 175 to record which warm-up exercises you have given to your students. Or distribute copies of the sheet for students to keep their own records. Use the certificate on page 176 as you see fit; for example, you can use the certificate as a reward for students who complete a certain amount of warm-up exercises.

How to Make the Most of This Book

✏ Read each lesson ahead of time before you use it with the class so that you are familiar with it. This will make it easier to answer students' questions.

✏ Set aside 10 to 12 minutes at a specific time daily to incorporate *Daily Warm-Ups: Nonfiction Reading* into your routine.

✏ Make sure the time you spend working on the materials is positive and constructive. This should be a time of practicing for success and recognizing it as it is achieved.

The passages and comprehension questions in *Daily Warm-Ups: Nonfiction Reading* are time-efficient, allowing your students to practice these skills often. The more your students practice reading and responding to content-area comprehension questions, the more confident and competent they will become.

Standards and Benchmarks

Each passage in *Daily Warm-Ups: Nonfiction Reading* meets at least one of the following standards and benchmarks, which are used with permission from McREL. Copyright 2011 McREL. Mid-continent Research for Education and Learning. 4601 DTC Boulevard, Suite 500, Denver, CO 80237. Telephone: 303-337-0990. Web site: *www.mcrel.org/standards-benchmarks*. Correlations to the Common Core State Standards can be found at *http://www.teachercreated.com/standards/*.

Uses the general skills and strategies of the reading process

- Establishes a purpose for reading
- Makes, confirms, and revises simple predictions about what will be found in a text
- Uses phonetic and structural analysis techniques, syntactic structure, and semantic context to decode unknown words
- Uses a variety of context clues to decode unknown words
- Understands level-appropriate reading vocabulary
- Monitors own reading strategies and makes modifications as needed
- Understands the author's purpose

Uses skills and strategies to read a variety of literary texts

- Reads a variety of literary passages and texts

Uses skills and strategies to read a variety of informational texts

- Reads a variety of informational texts
- Uses text organizers to determine the main ideas and to locate information in a text
- Summarizes and paraphrases information in texts
- Uses prior knowledge and experience to understand and respond to new information
- Understands structural patterns or organization in informational texts

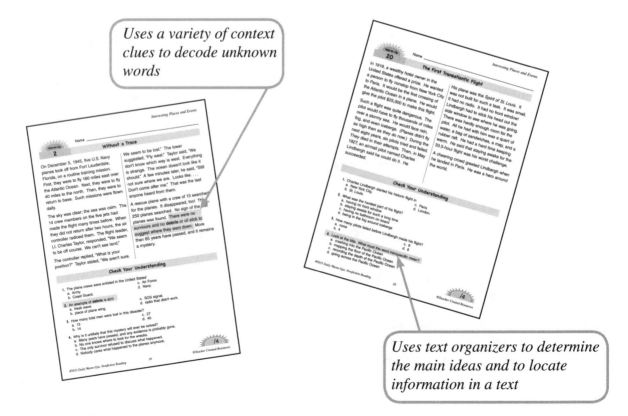

Uses a variety of context clues to decode unknown words

Uses text organizers to determine the main ideas and to locate information in a text

Interesting Places and Events

Warm-Up 1

Name _____

Racing to the South Pole

Roald Amundsen lived in Norway, and Robert Scott lived in England. Both men wanted to be the first to reach the South Pole. In January 1911, both men's teams landed in Antarctica. They set up base camps. Roald had his men build cairns. These piles of ice were guideposts to keep the men on the shortest route to the Pole. Each cairn held a note that told how to get to the next one.

The seasons in the Southern Hemisphere are the opposite of those in the Northern Hemisphere. While one has winter, the other has summer. So, October is spring in the Southern Hemisphere. That's when Roald and four of his men started out. At the end of November, they got caught in a blizzard that lasted for four days. It didn't stop them.

Roald had learned from the Inuit how to thrive in a very cold place. He knew that wearing two layers of fur keeps a person the warmest. He knew how to use a dog-sled team. He knew how to make dried meat. This knowledge is the reason he won the race. On December 14, 1911, Roald reached the South Pole. He left a tent with a note for Robert Scott. Then he and his men returned to base camp. The round trip had taken 39 days.

Check Your Understanding

1. Both Roald Amundsen and Robert Scott wanted to be the first to reach
   a. Antarctica.
   b. the cairns.
   c. the North Pole.
   d. the South Pole.

2. How long was Roald in Antarctica before starting his trek?
   a. 3 months
   b. 6 months
   c. 9 months
   d. one year

3. In Antarctica, it is spring. What season is it in Europe?
   a. spring
   b. summer
   c. fall
   d. winter

4. Why did Robert Scott lose the race?
   a. He was not as well prepared for the harsh conditions.
   b. He had a team of Inuit.
   c. He built cairns.
   d. He had less money than Roald Amundsen.

/4

Warm-Up
2

Name _____

Without a Trace

On December 5, 1945, five U.S. Navy planes took off from Fort Lauderdale, Florida, on a routine training mission. First, they were to fly 160 miles east over the Atlantic Ocean. Next, they were to fly 40 miles to the north. Then, they were to return to base. Such missions were flown daily.

The sky was clear; the sea was calm. The 14 crew members on the five jets had made the flight many times before. When they did not return after two hours, the air controller radioed them. The flight leader, Lt. Charles Taylor, responded, "We seem to be off course. We can't see land."

The controller replied, "What is your position?" Taylor stated, "We aren't sure. We seem to be lost." The tower suggested, "Fly west." Taylor said, "We don't know which way is west. Everything is strange. The ocean doesn't look like it should." A few minutes later, he said, "Still not sure where we are. Looks like. . . . Don't come after me." That was the last anyone heard from them.

A rescue plane with a crew of 13 searched for the planes. It disappeared, too! Then 250 planes searched. No sign of the lost planes was found. There were no survivors and no **debris** or oil slick to suggest where they went down. More than 65 years have passed, and it remains a mystery.

Check Your Understanding

1. The plane crews were enlisted in the United States'
   a. Army.
   b. Coast Guard.
   c. Air Force.
   d. Navy.

2. An example of **debris** is a(n)
   a. freak wave.
   b. piece of plane wing.
   c. SOS signal.
   d. radio that didn't work.

3. How many total men were lost in this disaster?
   a. 13
   b. 14
   c. 27
   d. 40

4. Why is it unlikely that this mystery will ever be solved?
   a. Many years have passed, and any evidence is probably gone.
   b. No one knows where to look for the wrecks.
   c. The only survivor refused to discuss what happened.
   d. Nobody cares what happened to the planes anymore.

/4

Name _____

Warm-Up 3 — Mysterious Rock Monuments

Easter Island lies off the coast of Chile in the South Pacific Ocean. The island is small but famous. It has many giant statues shaped like humans. They are hundreds of years old. People who lived there long ago made them. They may have been built to honor dead loved ones. These huge statues were carved by hand. Yet even with today's tools, this would be hard to do. Some statues have large, red rocks. They sit atop the heads like hats. Balancing those stones must have been hard—and dangerous.

In Great Britain, giant stone slabs tower over farm fields. They stand in a set of circles. What was this place? Who built it and why? The only thing we know for sure about Stonehenge is that it is thousands of years old. The amount of work to build it is shocking. Perhaps it acted as a calendar. People may have used it to identify the summer and winter solstices. Maybe the people used the stones as a reference point to keep track of the sun, stars, and moon. Some think that Stonehenge was a sacred place where religious rites were held.

Check Your Understanding

1. What is so amazing about both Easter Island and Stonehenge?
   a. Heavy stones were cut and put into place without power equipment.
   b. Ancient people were willing to die to defend the sites against attackers.
   c. There is proof that beings from space helped ancient people to construct each site.
   d. They prove that many ancient people practiced the same religion.

2. Stonehenge was most likely built as a
   a. calculator.
   b. cemetery.
   c. place for ceremonies.
   d. castle.

3. Which of these stone structures is the oldest?
   a. Stonehenge
   b. the Washington Monument in Washington, D.C.
   c. the statues on Easter Island
   d. a stone bridge built during the Civil War

4. Easter Island lies off the coast of which continent?
   a. Europe
   b. South America
   c. North America
   d. Asia

/4

Warm-Up 4

Name _____

Alaska, America's Final Frontier

In 1867, the United States bought Alaska from Russia. It is the biggest state. It is larger than California, Texas, and Montana put together! Canada separates Alaska from the rest of its nation.

Alaska is mostly wilderness. It has more than three million lakes and half of the world's glaciers. It has a long shore, too. More than half of the coastline of the whole United States is in Alaska! It has Mount McKinley, the continent's tallest peak. An island chain stretches from Alaska almost to Russia.

Few people live in Alaska. That may be because living there is different from living almost anywhere else. It is cold most of the time. A "hot" day may be 72°F. The state stays dark for about six months each year when the sun hardly rises in the sky. During the other six months, there is lots of daylight when the sun does not leave the sky. It stays bright at night.

It costs a lot to live in Alaska, too. Food and other goods must come from out of state. There are few roads. In fact, the capital city of Juneau can only be reached by ferry. Yet Alaska's rugged beauty brings in a lot of tourist dollars. More than 1.7 million people visit each year.

Check Your Understanding

1. What separates Alaska from the rest of the United States?
   a. Canada
   b. California
   c. Texas
   d. Montana

2. What does Alaska have half of all in the world?
   a. lakes
   b. glaciers
   c. coastline
   d. islands

3. Mount McKinley is the tallest mountain in
   a. Canada.
   b. Central America.
   c. South America.
   d. North America.

4. Why is it expensive to live in Alaska?
   a. Everyone has to have a car, a snowmobile, and a motorboat.
   b. There are no tourists.
   c. Most of the food has to be shipped in from far away.
   d. It is hard to sleep for half the year.

 /4

Warm-Up 5

Name _____

The First Climb Up Mount Everest

Mount Everest is Earth's tallest mountain. It is 5.5 miles high. The air is so thin at the top that each breath hurts. Hurricane-force winds blow past the peak. The cold threatens noses and limbs with frostbite.

Until 1953, no one had ever climbed Everest and lived to tell the tale. Then, Edmund Hillary of New Zealand and Tenzing Norgay of Nepal made history. Their spiked boots dug into the snow as they started up the mountain. Along the way, the men set up nine camps. They rested in each one for days. During that time, their bodies doubled their red blood cells. This let their blood carry more oxygen. Above 26,000 feet, the men used oxygen tanks. This saved their lives.

Altitude sickness can kill by letting one's lungs slowly fill with fluid.

The Lhotse Face is a 4,000-foot wall of ice. If one of the men had lost his footing on it, he would have slid for a mile. Then he would have fallen into a deep crack! It took the men two days to climb this part. Then, they made their last camp. They started at dawn on May 29. Around noon, they stood on the summit. They took photos. But they stayed just a few minutes. They had a six-hour trip back. They made it to camp just before dark.

Check Your Understanding

1. The last names of the first men to reach the peak of Mount Everest are
   a. Edmund and Tenzing.
   b. Edmund and Norgay.
   c. Hillary and Norgay.
   d. Tenzing and Hillary.

2. Why did the men use oxygen during their climb?
   a. to double their red blood cells
   b. to keep from sliding down the Lhotse Face
   c. to stay warm
   d. to prevent altitude sickness

3. Why did the men set up nine base camps?
   a. to avoid climbing the Lhotse Face
   b. to let their bodies get used to the different heights
   c. to keep themselves from overheating
   d. to reduce the amount of time they had to spend on the mountain

4. How long ago did these men climb Mount Everest?
   a. about 25 years ago
   b. about 40 years ago
   c. more than 55 years ago
   d. more than 85 years ago

/4

Warm-Up

6

Name _____

The Triangle Shirtwaist Fire

The Triangle Shirtwaist Company was in New York City. March 25, 1911, started out like any other day. It was a payday. Near quitting time, paychecks were handed to the workers on the tenth floor. Most were teenage girls. Many were immigrants. They sewed shirts for low pay. They trudged up the stairs to get their checks.

Suddenly, a fire broke out on the tenth floor. The stairs could not let all the women pass. Very few got out. The only fire escape was attached to the side of the building. When the women stepped onto it, it fell to the ground! Some girls waited at the windows for the firemen. But their ladders could not reach that high. Water from the hoses did not reach the tenth floor, either.

The trapped girls were scared of being burned alive. They chose to leap to their deaths instead. A total of 146 died. There was a second exit that could have saved lives, but it had been nailed shut. The owners had worried someone would steal spools of thread.

The loss of life was terrible. Yet some good came from this tragedy. It brought about laws that required safer working conditions.

Check Your Understanding

1. Why were nearly all the workers on the tenth floor at the same time?
   a. They all worked on that floor.
   b. They were there to get their pay.
   c. They were applying for a job.
   d. They were there for a company meeting.

2. People were angry because the Triangle Shirtwaist owners
   a. caused the fire.
   b. refused to let anyone fight the fire.
   c. did not pay the workers enough money.
   d. cared more about theft than their workers' safety.

3. Why did so many girls jump from the building?
   a. They planned to land on the fire escape.
   b. They thought the firemen would catch them.
   c. They were desperate to escape the flames.
   d. There was a portable trampoline on which they could land.

4. Which is an example of a law that resulted from the Triangle Shirtwaist fire?
   a. Employers must pay workers the minimum wage.
   b. Employers must have enough fire exits for workers to get out quickly.
   c. Employers must offer their workers a five-day workweek.
   d. Employers must offer their workers paid sick time.

/4

Warm-Up
7

Name _____

Saved by the Ringtones

An avalanche happens when snow high on a mountain begins to slide. As it slides, it knocks tons more snow loose. That snow also slides down the mountain. This wall of snow can move 100 miles per hour. It can knock down full-grown trees. Some avalanches have buried whole towns.

Often people get buried under the avalanche. They were skiing or snowboarding when the wall of snow hit them. They get so confused that they don't know which way to dig to reach the surface. Yet they will run out of air if they don't get out from under the snow quickly. Dogs search for them. With their keen sense of smell, dogs can check a snow-covered area fast. Once the dogs find the area, rescuers use long poles called avalanche probes. They stick them in the snow to find the person's exact location. Then they dig as fast as they can. Each second counts. The faster the victim gets oxygen and warmth, the higher the chances the person will live.

In 2010, avalanches happened along a road in Afghanistan. They caused the death of more than 165 people. The snow buried buses and cars. The area to search was huge. Cell phones saved some of the survivors. The searchers heard the phones ringing. They dug in those places.

Check Your Understanding

1. What do most people die from in an avalanche?
   a. They run out of air to breathe.
   b. They bleed to death.
   c. They drown.
   d. They starve.

2. Why do searchers use avalanche probes?
   a. The probes are more reliable than dogs.
   b. The probes bring air to buried people.
   c. The probes can find electronic devices.
   d. The probes let them find right where the people are under the snow.

3. How did ringtones save avalanche victims in Afghanistan?
   a. The cell phones sent GPS signals to a satellite.
   b. The cell phone ringtones melted the snow around the victim.
   c. Searchers dug where they heard cell phones ringing.
   d. Victims used their cell phones to dig themselves out of the snow.

4. Why are avalanche victims often unable to help themselves?
   a. They dig so fast that they get overheated and faint.
   b. They have tossed and tumbled so much that they don't know which way is up.
   c. They forget to call for help.
   d. They don't realize the danger they are in.

/4

Name _____

Warm-Up 8 — The Galveston Hurricane of 1900

The deadliest natural disaster in U.S. history occurred in 1900. It happened in Galveston, Texas. It is a small island just two miles wide and 25 miles long. It lies in the Gulf of Mexico off the Texas coast. A strong hurricane struck. It killed more than 10,000 people.

The U.S. Weather Bureau knew about the hurricane. A man raised two flags on a pole atop the Weather Bureau building. One flag meant that a bad storm was coming. The other told its direction. The people knew what these flags meant. But many did not want to leave. Those who stayed made a mistake.

A hurricane causes a storm surge. It is like a big wall of water. It hits the shore before the rest of the storm. The storm surge was 20 feet above sea level. And the city was just five feet above sea level. The whole island flooded. Water turned the soil to mud. Some buildings tilted. Others caved in. The bridges joining the island to the mainland washed away. Then the storm struck. High winds tore off roofs. Waves pounded the city. Docks crumbled. Sixteen ships were in the harbor. They sailed through the city and smashed into things.

Since then, Galveston has faced more hurricanes. Now a stone seawall protects it from storm surges.

Check Your Understanding

1. How many ships sailed into the city during the storm?
   a. 5
   b. 16
   c. 20
   d. 25

2. Why is Galveston safer today than before the hurricane of 1900?
   a. No one has lived on the island since that hurricane.
   b. People have built hurricane-proof houses and buildings on the island.
   c. People are warned about hurricanes now, and they weren't in 1900.
   d. There is a seawall built around the island.

3. How much higher than sea level was the storm surge compared to the city of Galveston?
   a. 5 feet
   b. 15 feet
   c. 20 feet
   d. 25 feet

4. The most destructive part of the Galveston Hurricane in 1900 was the
   a. lightning.
   b. rain.
   c. flooding.
   d. high winds.

/4

Warm-Up
9

Name _____

The Bridge that Lasted Four Months

When the Tacoma Narrows Bridge was built, it was the third-longest suspension bridge in the world. It crossed Puget Sound in Washington. The bridge had two main towers. A series of cables held up the roadway. Traffic started crossing the bridge on July 1, 1940. Soon people said that there was something wrong with the bridge. It moved up and down on windy days. They called it "Galloping Gertie." But the bridge's designers said it was safe. It could carry **enormous** weight. That fact turned out to be true. Yet the bridge was not safe.

A strong wind blew on the morning of November 7, 1940. It made the bridge move up and down in a flowing, wave-like motion. One man lost control of his car on the wildly rocking bridge. He got out. He crawled toward a tower. Then the bridge caved in. His car fell into the water below. He ran the rest of the way. He made it off the bridge. The wind had caused a "standing wave." It tore the bridge apart. There are videos of the bridge falling apart on the Web.

In 1950, a new suspension bridge was built in the same spot. People call it Sturdy Gertie. To handle more traffic, a second span was built in 2007.

Check Your Understanding

1. Why do you think people complained about the bridge from the start?
   a. On windy days, the bridge moved up and down.
   b. On windy days, the bridge swayed from side to side.
   c. On windy days, the bridge twisted and turned.
   d. On windy days, the bridge would get large cracks.

2. The antonym of the word **enormous** is
   a. huge.   b. unknown.   c. tiny.   d. less.

3. Why did the man trapped on the bridge crawl to a tower?
   a. It was hard to keep his balance enough to walk on the moving bridge.
   b. He had been in a wheelchair, but it had fallen through the hole in the bridge.
   c. He didn't know how to walk.
   d. He was too afraid to walk.

4. You can conclude that
   a. designers immediately built the same bridge again.
   b. designers figured out what went wrong before rebuilding the bridge.
   c. people decided that it was too dangerous to build any bridge there.
   d. people realized that a suspension bridge wouldn't work there.

/4

Warm-Up

10

Deadly Mudflows in South America

Name _____

On May 31, 1970, a strong earthquake shook the town of Yungay, Peru. Streets cracked. Buildings fell down. But most of the people survived. Then they heard a rumble. It came from the slopes of the nation's tallest mountain.

When the quake shook the mountain, it tore loose millions of tons of rock, snow, and ice. They slid down and crashed into lakes. The lakes burst from their banks. A wave of mud, ice, and rocks rushed toward the town. It moved 180 miles per hour. It took just three minutes for it to go 10 miles. No one had time to get away. Tons of ice, mud, and rock buried the town. Most of the 20,000 people who lived there died. Just 92 people on the far edge of the town survived.

Volcanoes can cause deadly mudflows, too. In November 1985, a volcano erupted in Colombia. The ice covering the mountain melted fast. It mixed with ash and dirt to form mud. The mud raced down the side of the mountain toward a town 40 miles away. The town leader warned the people. He told them to climb a nearby hill. But most people did not want to go out in the rain. While they slept, the mudflow gushed into town. It buried everything under a deep layer of mud. More than 25,000 people died that night.

Check Your Understanding

1. The mudflow that buried Yungay, Peru, started because of a(n)
   a. heavy snowfall.
   b. loud noise.
   c. volcano.
   d. earthquake.

2. About how many total people died in both disasters?
   a. 20,000
   b. 25,000
   c. 45,000
   d. 100,000

3. Which event occurred first?
   a. An earthquake hit Peru.
   b. People were buried in their sleep by a mudflow.
   c. A volcano erupted in Colombia.
   d. People were buried under tons of ice, rock, and mud.

4. Why did so few people listen to Colombia's town leader?
   a. They didn't believe the volcano had erupted.
   b. They thought they were too far away for the volcano to affect them.
   c. They didn't realize the danger of a mudflow.
   d. They thought the rain was more dangerous than a mudflow.

/4

Warm-Up

11   The Mysterious Rocks of Racetrack Playa

Name _____

Death Valley is a desert in California. One part of the desert, Racetrack Playa, is the dry bed of what was once a lake. The sun has baked the dirt of Racetrack Playa to a rock-like hardness. Rocks and boulders lie all over it. These rocks slide across the ground. Some move a few inches. Others move several yards. The rocks often leave paths. Some paths are straight, others loop and twist, and a few even go backwards. No one knows why.

Since the ground is flat, the rocks cannot be sliding downhill. Some people think that the night dew makes the ground slick. Then wind pushes the stones across the mud. Yet the rocks have moved at times when there was no wind. Some of the stones have iron in them, so scientists suggested that there might be a magnetic force under the ground. However, that does not make sense. Once when three rocks were close together, two of them moved in opposite directions. The third didn't move at all.

Strangest of all, no one has ever seen the rocks move. Nor are there any videos. However, scientists do keep charts of the stones' positions. That's how they know that one of them has moved 659 feet!

Check Your Understanding

1. Where is Racetrack Playa located?
   a. in a desert in California
   b. along the West Coast in California
   c. in a valley in California
   d. near a lake in California

2. What mystery surrounds the Racetrack Playa rocks?
   a. There should be no rocks in this area.
   b. No one can figure out what's making the rocks move.
   c. There are videos showing the rocks sliding around by themselves.
   d. The rocks contain elements that only come from outer space.

3. We know for sure that the rocks are moving because
   a. many people have seen them slide.
   b. there are videos of them sliding.
   c. they all leave paths.
   d. there are written records of their changing positions.

4. Scientists are sure that the rocks are *not* being moved by
   a. minor earthquakes.
   b. strong winds.
   c. gravity.
   d. magnetic force.

/4

Name _____

12   The First Moon Landing

On July 20, 1969, Neil Armstrong climbed down a ladder. Millions of people watched him on their television sets. As he stepped off the ladder, he said, "That's one small step for man, one giant leap for mankind." Neil was the first human to set foot on our moon. A movie camera was mounted on the spaceship. It showed his first step.

Neil was an astronaut on the *Apollo 11* mission. Because the moon has no air, he wore a spacesuit that gave him oxygen. His spacesuit weighed 180 pounds! The moon has less gravity than Earth. So there it weighed just 30 pounds. Neil felt so light on the moon that he jumped high.

Neil looked at some of the moon's craters. One is so big that a city the size of London, England, could fit inside it! Space rocks called meteors had slammed into the moon and formed these craters.

Neil gathered rocks for scientists to study. He put up the U.S. flag with wires sewn along the top and bottom edges. This made the flag look like it was flying. Otherwise it would have been limp. There is no wind on the moon.

Check Your Understanding

1. Neil Armstrong was a(n)
   a. doctor.
   b. teacher.
   c. astronaut.
   d. movie star.

2. When he stood on the moon, Neil felt
   a. heavier than he did on Earth.
   b. lighter than he did on Earth.
   c. the same weight as he did on Earth.
   d. like he couldn't move his limbs.

3. What did Neil leave on the moon?
   a. a television set
   b. a movie camera
   c. his spacesuit
   d. a flag

4. The moon has craters because
   a. it has been struck by meteors.
   b. a U.S. spacecraft caused them.
   c. Neil removed so many rocks that he left big holes.
   d. it bumped into Earth millions of years ago.

/4

Warm-Up

13

Name _____

The Klondike Gold Rush

In 1896, a man found gold in the Klondike. It is an area in the far west of Canada. He and two friends mined all winter. In the spring, ships carried the men's gold. They sailed to Washington and California. That's when people outside the Klondike heard about it. Thousands rushed there. Even Seattle's mayor quit his job to go there! Most of the people took ships to Skagway. Then they had a choice: follow White Pass Trail or Chilkoot Trail. Both ended at Lake Bennett. From there, people built rafts. They sailed 500 miles down the Yukon River.

White Pass Trail was 45 miles long. It had narrow ledges along cliffs. Boulders and logs blocked some parts. Chilkoot Pass was 12 miles shorter. But it was so steep that horses couldn't do it. Miners had to carry all their own supplies. They weighed one ton! Miners broke this down into 20 packs of 100 pounds each. They walked the same path 20 times to move all their gear! It took a long time to get to the end of the "shorter" trail.

About 100,000 people headed to the Klondike. Just 40,000 made it all the way there. About 300 got rich.

Check Your Understanding

1. What is the name of the river on which miners had to travel to get to the gold fields?
   a. Yukon
   b. Skagway
   c. Chilkoot
   d. Klondike

2. Why did some miners choose Chilkoot Pass?
   a. They could use horses to carry their supplies.
   b. It was less steep than White Pass Trail.
   c. It was a shorter trail.
   d. It was much faster than taking White Pass Trail.

3. Seattle's mayor quit because he wanted to
   a. be the mayor of Klondike.
   b. lead people into the wilderness.
   c. be the captain of a ship carrying gold rushers.
   d. find gold in Canada.

4. Most of the people who headed to the Klondike
   a. struck it rich.
   b. did not even make it all the way there.
   c. stayed in the area for the rest of their lives.
   d. chose to follow White Pass Trail.

/4

Warm-Up
14

Name _____

The Lake on the Mountain

The Lake on the Mountain is a natural wonder. It is in Ontario, Canada. Although water always flows to the lowest point, this lake lies 203 feet above the Bay of Quinte. In one spot, the lake's water crashes down a waterfall and flows to the bay. Yet the lake's depth stays the same! There isn't enough rain to keep its level constant. So there must be springs under the lake.

How did the lake form? Some say that a meteor hit the mountain. It left a deep hole. Over time, it filled from springs and rain. Others say that it is the crater of an old volcano. This idea fits Native-American tales. These stories called it a "smoking mountain." (In other places, water has filled old volcano craters.)

Most people think that the lake formed the way that underground caves do. Carbon dioxide in the air mixed with rain. This formed an acid. After a long time, it wore away the limestone. It formed a hole.

The Lake on the Mountain is a park. Many people visit it each year. They want to see for themselves that there really is a Lake on the Mountain.

Check Your Understanding

1. The Lake on the Mountain
   a. has a waterfall.
   b. is fed by a river.
   c. has a whirlpool in its center.
   d. is kept filled by melting snow.

2. The Lake on the Mountain may have formed by
   a. humans digging a huge pit.
   b. an explosion.
   c. an earthquake.
   d. a volcano.

3. The depth of the lake
   a. is rising.
   b. is falling.
   c. stays about the same.
   d. changes all the time.

4. The Lake on the Mountain is located in
   a. Europe.
   b. Australia.
   c. North America.
   d. South America.

/4

Warm-Up

15

Name _____

A Perfect Emergency Landing

On January 15, 2009, the world saw its first perfect emergency water landing of a jet plane. The plane landed in the icy cold water of the Hudson River in New York City. The plane had taken off less than one minute before. A flock of geese flew into both engines. The engines quit. The plane was going down.

The plane lost **altitude** fast. The pilot, Chelsey "Sully" Sullenberger, knew he could not reach the airport. So he guided the damaged plane into the water. The plane hit the water gently. It did not break apart. But it did start to sink. The people rushed to get out. They stood on the wings. They were knee-deep in the water.

The air was 20°F. The water was 36°F. That's just four degrees above freezing.

Coast Guard boats and a ferry were close by. They rushed to help. The passengers were in danger. If their body temperatures dropped too low, they could die. In the cold, it could take just five minutes for that to happen.

All 155 aboard survived the landing. In every other crash landing in water, the jet has broken apart. Some—and usually most—of those onboard have died.

Check Your Understanding

1. The Hudson River flows through
   a. an airport.
   b. New York City.
   c. North Carolina.
   d. New Jersey.

2. The word **altitude** means
   a. steering ability.
   b. length of the plane's wings.
   c. weight of the plane's cargo.
   d. height above Earth.

3. What made this emergency landing so remarkable?
   a. Nobody died.
   b. The plane broke into pieces.
   c. People called it a miracle.
   d. Birds had flown into both of the plane's engines.

4. Even after the plane had landed safely, the people aboard still faced the danger of
   a. being swept out to sea.
   b. getting too cold.
   c. bleeding to death.
   d. breaking bones.

/4

Warm-Up

16

Colorado River Adventure

Name _____

The Colorado River carved out the Grand Canyon. It took millions of years. The rushing water carried sand and pebbles. They ground away at the rock walls. This formed a gorge one mile deep.

The Colorado River has many waterfalls and rapids. The water speeds up where the river narrows. Boaters must steer around rocks. If a person falls out of the boat, he may be smashed against rocks. Rapids are rated Class 1 to 6. Class 5 rapids have huge waves and jagged rocks. The Colorado River has lots of Class 5 and 6 rapids. Most Class 6 rapids cannot be run.

The river had never been run until 1869. That year, John Wesley Powell and 10 men set out. They had four wooden boats. They took 10 months of food and gear. They would go 1,000 miles through uncharted wilderness.

When they heard the roar of upcoming rapids, Powell made the men get out. They carried the heavy boats and gear along the rocky shore. But sometimes the river took charge. It swept the boats through raging rapids while the men hung on.

One month into the trip, the group had lost one boat and much of their supplies. Four men quit along the way. After three months, Powell and the rest of the team finished their wild ride.

Check Your Understanding

1. Why did Powell and his team run the Colorado River?
   a. They wanted to sell maps of the river's course.
   b. They wanted to start a whitewater rafting business.
   c. They wanted to be the first people to do it.
   d. They wanted to get rich.

2. Why did they sometimes carry their boats?
   a. They thought that the rapids ahead were too dangerous to ride.
   b. There were dangerous winds blowing through the gorge.
   c. They feared losing their gear in the water.
   d. They needed the physical exercise.

3. When a river has a waterfall, that part of the river is most likely a Class
   a. 3.   b. 4.   c. 5.   d. 6.

4. You can tell that Powell
   a. was always in control of the boats and the men.
   b. wasn't always in control of the boats and the men.
   c. had no idea how to run the river.
   d. was afraid of taking risks.

/4

Name _____

The High Desert

A rain-shadow desert forms on one side of a mountain range. There is a big one in the United States. It covers 20 percent of the nation's land. This desert lies in parts of Washington, Oregon, and California. It is part of Idaho, Montana, Wyoming, Nevada, and Utah. It covers parts of Canada, too. It is called the high desert.

In the summer, the high desert is hot and dry. In the winter, it is cold. The spring may have flash floods. What causes this weather pattern? The Sierra Nevadas and the Cascade Mountains do. They stand between the Pacific Ocean and the high desert. Rain clouds form over the sea. Winds move the clouds east. The clouds hit the west side of the tall mountains.

They drop their rain. The rain does not make it to the other side of the mountains. So the western side of these mountains has lush green forests. The eastern side gets less than 20 inches of rain and snow each year. When rain does fall, it may fall fast. Then there's a flood. The ground cannot soak up the water fast enough.

The plants and animals that live in the high desert have adapted to these conditions. Ponderosa pine, bunchgrass, and shrubs live there. Lizards, great horned owls, and kangaroo rats are at home there, too.

Check Your Understanding

1. How many states in the United States are part of a rain-shadow desert?
   a. 3
   b. 5
   c. 8
   d. 20

2. In a rain-shadow desert, you wouldn't be likely to see
   a. tall trees.
   b. frogs.
   c. shrubs.
   d. lizards.

3. A rain-shadow desert always lies
   a. on one side of a mountain range.
   b. on both sides of a mountain range.
   c. along an ocean coast.
   d. between a mountain range and a cold desert.

4. What could cause a flood in the high desert?
   a. Glaciers melt on the mountains.
   b. Wind patterns can change, bringing lots of rain to the area.
   c. Hurricanes strike this area frequently.
   d. When rain falls, the ground can't absorb it fast enough.

/4

Name _____

Warm-Up

18   Finding a Missing Masterpiece

In her life, Nella Jones had never seen the painting *The Guitar Player* by Jan Vermeer. It is a famous masterpiece painted in the 1600s. It shows a seated girl playing a guitar. The painting is worth a lot of money. In 1974, it was worth 4.8 million dollars. It was stolen from the Kenwood House Museum in London, England.

Nella had a vision about the stolen painting. It seemed so real that she called the police. She told them that the thieves had taken the painting out of its frame. The frame was heavy. It made it hard to carry. She told them where to find the frame. And when the police found it there, Nella was in trouble! They thought she had stolen the painting.

A newspaper called *The Times* received a ransom letter. The thieves wanted the Price sisters set free from jail and taken to Northern Ireland. They didn't get their demand. Ten weeks after it vanished, Nella was ironing clothes while watching TV. Suddenly, she saw the painting in her mind. It was in a churchyard. She didn't know the place. Still, she drew a sketch for the police of what the church looked like. The police found the painting on the church grounds. Luckily, it was not damaged from being left outdoors.

Check Your Understanding

1. *The Guitar Player* was painted by
   a. Nella Jones.
   b. Jan Vermeer.
   c. the Price sisters.
   d. an anonymous artist in the 1600s.

2. What did the thieves want in exchange for the painting's return?
   a. the Price sisters let out of jail
   b. $4.8 million
   c. Nella Jones to predict where they had left the painting
   d. to own the Kenwood House Museum

3. Why were the police suspicious of Nella Jones?
   a. They had physical evidence that tied her to the theft.
   b. She knew where to find the painting's frame.
   c. She was related to the Price sisters.
   d. She said she knew the thieves' names but refused to tell the police.

4. Why did Nella contact the police twice?
   a. She hoped they would pay her for the information she had.
   b. She had a guilty conscience because she had helped the thieves.
   c. She wanted to prove her innocence.
   d. She wanted to help them find the frame and the painting.

/4

Name _____

The Everglades

Some people think that Florida's Everglades is a huge swamp. It's not. It is the world's biggest marsh. It has tall grass, short trees, and shallow water. In most places, the water's fresh. Near the ocean, it's brackish. That means it is a mix of salt and fresh water. Some animals can only live in this kind of water.

People built canals and took the water. They used it for drinking, cleaning, and watering crops. People drained other areas and put buildings up. This has cut down on the Everglades' size. Now the plants and animals living there are in danger. The most endangered animals are crocodiles, panthers, and frogs.

Florida has an **ambitious** plan to help the Everglades. It will probably take 50 years to do. First, they will dig deep wells. The wells will tap the groundwater for the people living there. Next, they will remove the canals. Then more water will flow through the Everglades, as it did in the past.

But that won't fix every problem. People got snakes as pets. Then they got tired of them. They let them go in the Everglades! The snakes killed the native animals. They took native snakes' food. So people are removing them. In 2009, 367 Burmese pythons were taken from the Everglades.

Check Your Understanding

1. Which event did not harm the Everglades?
   a. People removed water from the Everglades with canals.
   b. People released pet Burmese pythons into the Everglades.
   c. People decided to use groundwater instead of water from the Everglades.
   d. People built buildings on land that had once been part of the Everglades.

2. Which kind of animal will benefit from Florida's new plan?
   a. coyotes
   b. turtles
   c. camels
   d. penguins

3. Florida wants to help the Everglades in order to
   a. keep the plants and animals there from becoming extinct.
   b. provide more fresh water for people to drink and irrigate crops.
   c. improve the area so that it can handle more tourists.
   d. find a way to use brackish water.

4. In this passage, the word **ambitious** means
   a. inexpensive.
   b. requiring much effort.
   c. overwhelming.
   d. impossible.

/4

Name _____

The First Transatlantic Flight

In 1919, a wealthy hotel owner in the United States offered a prize. He wanted a person to fly nonstop from New York City to Paris. It would be the first crossing of the Atlantic Ocean in a plane. He would give the pilot $25,000 to make this flight.

Such a flight was quite dangerous. The pilot would have to fly thousands of miles over a stormy sea. He would face rain, fog, and even icebergs. (Planes didn't fly as high then as they do now.) During the next eight years, six pilots tried and failed. They died in their attempts. Then, in May 1927, an airmail pilot named Charles Lindbergh said he could do it. He succeeded.

His plane was the *Spirit of St. Louis*. It was not built for such a task. It was small. It had no radio. It had no front window! Lindbergh had to stick his head out the side window to see where he was going. There was hardly enough room for the pilot. All he had with him was a quart of water, a bag of sandwiches, a map, and a rubber raft. He had a hard time keeping warm. He said that staying awake for the 33.5-hour flight was his worst challenge.

A cheering crowd greeted Lindbergh when he landed in Paris. He was a hero around the world.

Check Your Understanding

1. Charles Lindbergh started his historic flight in
   a. New York City.
   b. St. Louis.
   c. Paris.
   d. London.

2. What was the hardest part of his flight?
   a. having no front window
   b. staying awake for such a long time
   c. having no bathroom on board
   d. being in the fog around icebergs

3. How many pilots failed before Lindbergh made his flight?
   a. none
   b. 4
   c. 6
   d. 8

4. Look at the title. What must the word *transpacific* mean?
   a. crashing into the Pacific Ocean
   b. mapping the floor of the Pacific Ocean
   c. recording the depth of the Pacific Ocean
   d. going across the Pacific Ocean

/4

Warm-Up 21

Name _____

The City of Water

The city of Venice, Italy, has no streets. It has canals. It is built on a group of 118 islands. A network of canals and 400 bridges join these islands. From the air, no land can be seen. Venice seems to rise right out of the Adriatic Sea.

The islands are little more than sandbars. So why did anyone build there? A war in the 400s caused people to flee the mainland. They felt safer on the islands. If an attack came, they could get in boats and sail away. Over time, they built a city. Each building stands on sturdy wood posts. These posts were sunk deep into the sand. The people traded with merchants from Asia.

In the 1400s, Venice was one of the richest cities on Earth. Each year, about 3,000 ships visited its ports. By the 1700s, Venice was no longer an important port. Yet it has remained a center of music, art, and theater. Now more than 15 million tourists visit each year. They ride around the city in gondolas. They are long, narrow boats. A person using one long oar pushes it.

Venice has had floods. The sea level is rising. Now the MOSE project is being built. It will cost $4.5 billion. It should be done in 2014. Its 78 floodgates will keep water from drowning the city.

Check Your Understanding

1. Why did people build Venice?
   a. They wanted to be able to go out to sea very quickly.
   b. They wanted a city without any streets.
   c. They wanted a city like no other on Earth.
   d. They knew that annual floods would wash away their trash.

2. About how many people visit Venice annually?
   a. 5 million
   b. 15 million
   c. 45 million
   d. 118 million

3. Venice is
   a. a nation.
   b. one big island.
   c. part of Italy.
   d. underwater for about half of each year.

4. What is the MOSE project's purpose?
   a. to keep Venice clean
   b. to provide fresh water for the rising population
   c. to protect the city from invaders
   d. to keep the city from flooding

/4

Warm-Up
22

Name _____

The Dead Sea

You know that you cannot drink saltwater. If you drink a lot of saltwater, you will get thirstier and become ill. You must drink fresh water.

Can you guess how the Dead Sea got its name? Its water is so salty that *nothing* can live in it. It is almost nine times saltier than the ocean! The extra salt in the water isn't all bad, though. It makes it easy for people to float. Many people like to swim in the Dead Sea.

The Dead Sea lies between the nations of Israel and Jordan. This is a very dry area in the Middle East. It is uncommon for a body of water surrounded by land to be salty. The Dead Sea is strange in another way, too. Its surface and shores are 1,385 feet below sea level. That is the lowest point on Earth's surface.

The people living near the Dead Sea use its water for drinking and growing crops. First, they must put the water through a special process. It removes the salt. What is left is fresh water. Doing this costs a lot of money. Yet in a place where there's little water, people must use what's available. This is causing the water level to fall about three feet each year. At this rate, the Dead Sea may dry up within the next 50 years.

Check Your Understanding

1. Most bodies of water surrounded by land are
   a. polluted.
   b. unable to support living things.
   c. fresh water.
   d. saltwater.

2. The Dead Sea is located in the
   a. middle of a desert in Australia.
   b. Middle East.
   c. United States.
   d. driest part of Africa.

3. What is the main idea of this passage?
   a. People find it easy to float and swim in the salty Dead Sea.
   b. It is not healthy for people to drink saltwater.
   c. Although the Dead Sea is salty, people have found a way to use its water.
   d. The Dead Sea is unique because it is so salty and the lowest point on Earth.

4. How do the people use water from the Dead Sea for their crops?
   a. They change it into fresh water first.
   b. The plants in their area are used to saltwater and therefore are not harmed by it.
   c. They add it to fertilizer.
   d. They add chemicals to the soil to counteract the salt in the water.

/4

Warm-Up

23

Name _____

Earth's Hot Spots

Did you know that Yellowstone National Park lies above one of Earth's "hot spots"? A hot spot is where melted rock from Earth's mantle comes close to its crust. High heat turns water under the ground into steam. This hot water and steam blows up through holes. These places are called *geysers*. There are about 600 on Earth. And more than half of those are in Yellowstone.

A geyser is like a rock "pipe." The pipe stretches down to a reservoir that holds hot ground water. As the heat builds up, the water turns to steam. It needs to escape, just as steam does from a teakettle. As soon as there is enough steam, it shoots up the tube. It spurts into the air like a fountain.

Some geysers explode every couple of days. Others do so after years. They cannot be predicted. However, one Yellowstone geyser, Old Faithful, erupts several times a day in a regular pattern. It has done so for hundreds of years. Each time it erupts for about four minutes.

Hot springs lie above hot spots, too. There are places in Japan and Iceland where people can soak in a natural "hot tub" year round. The people do not get burned because the hot water mixes with cooler water near the ground's surface.

Check Your Understanding

1. Which one lies under a hot spring?
   a. a fountain
   b. a geyser
   c. a river
   d. a hot spot

2. How are geysers and volcanoes alike?
   a. Both send out lava.
   b. Both erupt from heat that comes from below the ground.
   c. Both cause hot springs to form.
   d. Both erupt in predictable patterns.

3. A geyser erupting looks most like
   a. a whistling teakettle.
   b. steam rising from a hot spring.
   c. a tall fountain.
   d. a waterfall.

4. Which place does not have any hot spots?
   a. Japan
   b. Iceland
   c. Yellowstone National Park
   d. not mentioned in passage

/4

Warm-Up

24

Name _____

The *Hindenburg* Disaster

Airships are also called blimps. They float because they are filled with a gas that is lighter than air. The gas used can be hydrogen or helium. In the early part of the 1900s, blimps owned the skies. In May 1936, the *Hindenburg* offered the first transatlantic air service. This means it crossed the Atlantic Ocean. During one year, it carried hundreds of passengers. It flew thousands of miles. It had a perfect safety record. Then it had a terrible disaster. It was on May 6, 1937. It happened at Naval Air Station in New Jersey.

The blimp carried 36 passengers and 61 crew. It was coming in for a landing. It was to be tied to a tall post. But, at an altitude of about 200 feet, a fire started near the *Hindenburg's* stern (rear). No one knows why. In just 35 seconds, the airship fell to the ground. It was covered in flames. Just 12 passengers and 37 crew lived. And most of those were hurt.

The use of airships ended. People were afraid to get in blimps. It was from that moment that planes took over the skies. The disaster would not have occurred if the *Hindenburg* had been filled with helium. In fact, its makers had urged its use. Helium would not have exploded or caused a fire.

Check Your Understanding

1. The *Hindenburg* was filled with
   a. nitrogen.
   b. oxygen.
   c. hydrogen.
   d. helium.

2. The *Hindenburg* was destroyed by a
   a. lightning strike.
   b. child playing with matches.
   c. passenger who was smoking.
   d. fire that started from unknown causes.

3. How many total people survived this disaster?
   a. 12
   b. 37
   c. 49
   d. 61

4. Why did planes take over the skies after May 6, 1937?
   a. People thought that planes were faster.
   b. People thought that planes were safer.
   c. Planes had cheaper tickets.
   d. Planes had better-trained pilots.

/4

Name _____

25 Spooky Places in North Carolina

Two places in North Carolina have been in legends for hundreds of years. Scientists have explored and tested both places. But no one knows what causes the strange **phenomena**.

The Devil's Tramping Ground is a circle in which nothing has grown for hundreds of years. It is in a forest near Bennett. The ring is 40 feet wide. The North Carolina State Department of Agriculture tested the soil. It has no nutrients in it. But no one knows why. After all, this spot is in the midst of a forest. There are plenty of dead plants. Their decay should build up the soil. Yet each morning, the circle looks like it has been swept clean. An item left in the circle overnight will be outside it in the morning. No one has an explanation for what is happening.

The Brown Mountain lights have made people wonder for 800 years. Long ago, two Native-American tribes fought a bloody battle there. Ever since then, strange lights have appeared at night on the mountain. Thousands of people have seen them. There are videos on the Web. Usually the lights are white. Sometimes they are colored. Often the lights are still. Yet sometimes they move. No one lives on the mountain. There are no roads or electric lights on the mountain.

Check Your Understanding

1. Strange lights have been seen
   a. over the Devil's Tramping Ground.
   b. on Brown Mountain.
   c. in a forest near Bennett, North Carolina.
   d. in all the places above.

2. Why don't plants grow in the Devil's Tramping Ground?
   a. Someone stomps on any sprouts.
   b. It is too dark in that part of the forest.
   c. There are no nutrients in the soil.
   d. Strange lights make plant seeds unable to sprout.

3. A synonym for **phenomena** is
   a. noises.
   b. events.
   c. odors.
   d. visions.

4. The Brown Mountain lights may be the result of
   a. unusual conditions in the air.
   b. house lights.
   c. streetlights.
   d. truck headlights.

/4

Warm-Up
26

The World's Tallest Building

The world's tallest building is Burj Khalifa. It is a skyscraper in the Middle East. It stands in Dubai. Dubai is a city in the nation of United Arab Emirates. It is more than half a mile high! It is twice as tall as the Empire State Building in New York City. In fact, at 2,717 feet, it is the tallest thing humans have ever built. What is all that space used for? It's used for a mixture of hotel rooms, apartments, and offices.

Burj Khalifa holds a lot of world records, too. It is the building with the most floors. It has 160. It has the highest mosque (on the 158th floor). It has the highest swimming pool, too. It's on the 76th floor.

It has the tallest and fastest elevators, as well.

The building has an outdoor lookout deck. It is the highest in the world. Its name is At the Top. It opened in January 2010. However, it is located on the 124th floor, which is nowhere near the top.

This building knocked Taipei 101 off its pedestal. Located in Taiwan, it had been the world's tallest building. It had that honor for just three years. Its design has withstood high winds and earthquakes.

Check Your Understanding

1. How many floors does the Burj Khalifa have?
   a. 101
   b. 124
   c. 158
   d. 160

2. In what year did Burj Khalifa's observation deck open?
   a. 1999
   b. 2007
   c. 2008
   d. 2010

3. How tall is this building?
   a. 2,101 feet
   b. 2,458 feet
   c. 2,717 feet
   d. 2,801 feet

4. Right before Burj Khalifa was built, the tallest building on Earth was
   a. the Empire State Building.
   b. Taipei 101.
   c. United Arab Emirates.
   d. At the Top.

/4

Warm-Up
27

Name _____

The Battle of Midway Island

Pearl Harbor was a big U.S. naval base. The Japanese made a surprise attack on it on December 7, 1941. This wrecked many U.S. ships and planes. It nearly wiped out the American Navy. As a result, the United States entered World War II.

The Japanese attacked Midway Island in June 1942. It is in the Pacific Ocean. The United States had to keep the island safe. Otherwise, the Japanese would set up a base there. Then, they could attack Hawaii and the West Coast.

The Battle of Midway took place over four days. The Japanese had four aircraft carriers. The Americans had three. Planes could take off and land on these ships.

Planes fought most of the battle. When the planes needed fuel or bombs, they went back to their ships.

In the first three days, the Japanese shot down almost 100 U.S. planes. It looked as if they would win. Then some U.S. bombers burst from the cloud cover. They bombed the Japanese aircraft carriers. Three of their ships sank. The fourth was hit hard, too. The Americans lost one aircraft carrier. Many planes had to crash land in the sea. They had no ship to land on.

Before this, America had been losing the war in the Pacific. This was the first Japanese defeat.

Check Your Understanding

1. Aircraft carriers were important because they
   a. moved faster than any other kind of ship.
   b. could transport jets far from land bases.
   c. couldn't sink.
   d. carried large numbers of soldiers into battle.

2. On a historical timeline, what happened **second**?
   a. Four of the Japanese aircraft carriers were damaged or destroyed.
   b. The Japanese attacked Pearl Harbor.
   c. The Japanese shot down nearly 100 American planes over the Pacific Ocean.
   d. The Japanese attacked Midway Island.

3. Why did the United States defend Midway?
   a. The United States owned Midway Island.
   b. America had promised the Midway islanders that they would be protected from the Japanese.
   c. America couldn't afford to let their enemy have a place from which they could easily attack the mainland.
   d. The American government had a lot of gold stored on the island.

4. The United States entered World War II because the Japanese attacked
   a. Midway Island.
   b. a U.S. naval base.
   c. a U.S. aircraft carrier.
   d. 100 U.S. planes.

/4

Name _____

Where Is Atlantis?

A tale says that Atlantis was a continent. People lived there in cities. They had a fleet of ships. They were peaceful. Women and men had the same legal rights. But then, in 1500 BCE, it sank into the sea. About 300 BCE, a man named Plato first wrote the story. He thought Atlantis was real. He wrote that big explosions had occurred there. After that, the land vanished. Plato thought that Atlantis had been in the Atlantic Ocean.

For hundreds of years, people searched for the missing land. Some say that it was off the coast of Scandinavia. Others say it was an island in the Caribbean. Some claim it was part of the Canary Islands. These islands lie off the coast of Spain.

Others say that Atlantis never existed. The only thing all agree upon is that it was not as big as a continent.

Now scientists think that Atlantis may lie under the Aegean Sea. (This is part of the Mediterranean Sea.) About 3,500 years ago, land was there. The Minoans lived on it. Their society had all the features from the tale. Then its volcano blew up. It was the second-biggest eruption in human history. It made a huge hole in the island. Water flooded the land. A recent dig on an island in that area found a Minoan city. It is partly under the sea's surface.

Check Your Understanding

1. What is the main idea of this passage?
   a. Atlantis lies at the bottom of the Aegean Sea.
   b. According to a tale, there is a missing continent called Atlantis.
   c. People started searching for Atlantis immediately after its disappearance.
   d. Scientists think they have found the missing landmass of Atlantis.

2. Another good title is for this passage is
   a. "The Lost Continent of Atlantis."
   b. "Submarine Explores Atlantis."
   c. "Atlantis: Jewel of the Atlantic Ocean."
   d. "Has Atlantis Been Found?"

3. The name of the people who lived in Atlantis was probably the
   a. Atlantians.
   b. Minoans.
   c. Aegeans.
   d. Platos.

4. Why do scientists think they've figured out where Atlantis is?
   a. Newly found ancient writings tell right where it was located.
   b. Deep sea divers have found whole cities on the Aegean Sea's floor.
   c. They know about a society in that area that matched the story's features and disaster.
   d. A recent volcanic eruption caused Atlantis to rise back out of the sea.

/4

Name _____

What's Hidden on Oak Island?

Oak Island lies off the shore of Nova Scotia, Canada. For over 200 years, men have dug on this small island. They search for buried treasure. They think pirates hid some there.

In 1795, a 16-year-old boy and his friends found a shaft like a well. They began digging. Ninety feet underground, they found a big, flat stone. It had strange marks. When they removed it, water flooded the shaft.

Others kept up the search. Eleven tunnels have been dug. All that's been found is an ivory whistle, bits of iron and brass, and coconut fiber mats. The mats were carbon dated to 1200–1400 CE. But that tells when

the mats were made, not when they were put in the pit.

Some people think the pit holds the jewelry of the French queen Marie Antoinette. Before she died in 1793, she gave her maid her jewels. The maid sewed them into the lining of her skirts. Then the French Navy, which was loyal to the queen, took her to Canada and dug the pit.

People still search. Perhaps there is no treasure. Or maybe someone found it and took it without saying so. Many say that there was never a treasure. The pit is just a natural sinkhole.

Check Your Understanding

1. Why have people dug 11 tunnels on Oak Island?
   a. Each person is helping to build an underground maze.
   b. Each person is working on creating a flood-control system.
   c. Each person is hoping to be the one who finds the treasure.
   d. Each person is trying to convince others that there's treasure hidden there.

2. You can conclude that the pirates
   a. never hid anything on Oak Island.
   b. may have hidden something there about 150 years ago.
   c. may have hidden something there more than 200 years ago.
   d. stole Marie Antoinette's jewelry.

3. If someone already found and removed the treasure, what's the most probable reason that the person didn't say so?
   a. to watch everyone else continue to search in vain
   b. to avoid paying taxes on the value of the treasure
   c. to continue to make money as a guide who helps people search the island
   d. to keep Marie Antoinette from claiming the treasure

4. You can tell that
   a. many people are eager to find buried riches.
   b. treasure hunters are too lazy to get a real job.
   c. no one believes that there's a treasure on Oak Island.
   d. people will dig deeper on Oak Island until they reach Asia.

/4

Warm-Up

30

Name _____

The Great Race of Mercy

In January 1925, an outbreak of diphtheria hit Nome, Alaska. It was deadly. About 1,400 people were in danger. There was a cure. But the closest serum (medicine) was far away. The serum couldn't go by boat. Ice clogged the waterways. It couldn't go by plane. There was just one way for the serum to get there. Sled dogs had to carry it.

Just before midnight on January 27, the first musher (sled driver) and dog team began the race. The air was so cold that it could hurt the dogs' lungs. Two dogs died as a result. The dog teams averaged six miles an hour in brutal cold and darkness. (During winter in Alaska, the sun only shines for a few hours at midday.) A total of 20 mushers and 150 dogs ran around the clock. Each team carried the serum to the next team. They braved deadly temperatures. They faced icy winds and blinding snowstorms. They crossed thin ice with cracks. It took five and a half days to travel 674 miles. It would usually take more than two weeks to go that far.

The serum reached Nome on February 2. A doctor gave people the shots. Less than a dozen people died. Since 1973, the Iditarod Trail Sled Dog Race runs each year in March. It honors those who carried the serum.

Check Your Understanding

1. The people in Nome needed
   a. diphtheria.
   b. serum.
   c. musher.
   d. iditarod.

2. Each year, the Iditarod Race is held during
   a. January.
   b. February
   c. March.
   d. the same week as the original race.

3. The dog teams were *not* in danger from
   a. falling through ice.
   b. extreme heat.
   c. extreme cold.
   d. exhaustion.

4. A musher is the
   a. lead dog in a dog-sled team.
   b. medicine that cures diphtheria.
   c. sled that the dogs pull.
   d. person who drives a dog-sled team.

/4

Scientifically Speaking

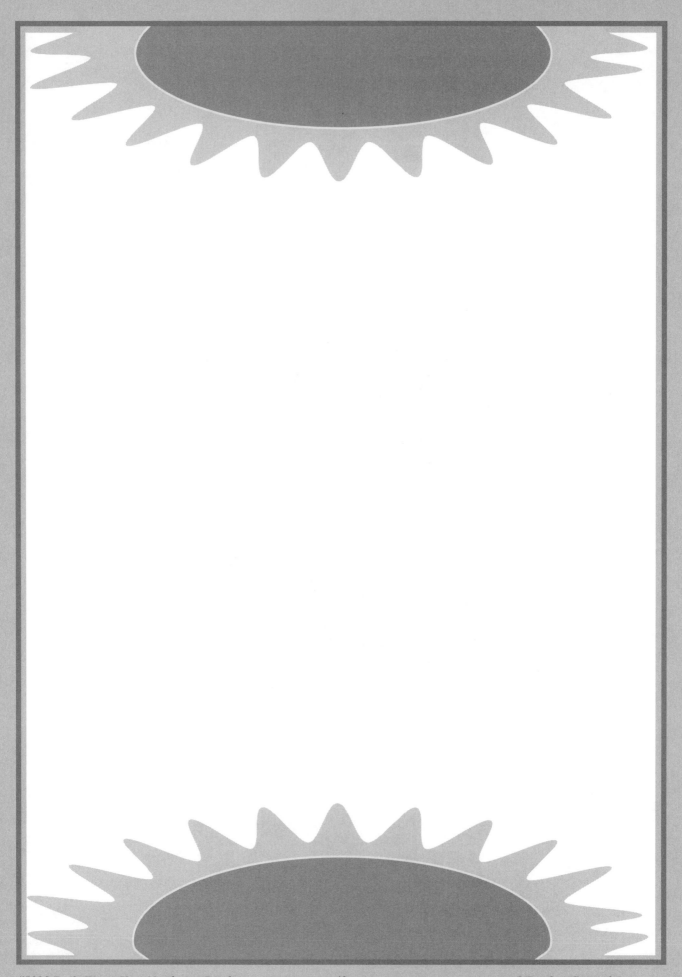

Warm-Up 1

Name _____

Your Genes

Do you have curly hair? Are you taller than other kids your age? These **characteristics** were decided before you were born. You got your traits from your parents. They passed their traits on to you through genes. (*Genes* is pronounced just like *jeans*.)

Genes carry the codes for blue eyes or brown eyes. Genes determine how tall you will get and what color hair you will have. You got half of your genes from your mother and half from your father. This means you have your own unique set of genes. Each person gets different genes for each body part. That is why you may look similar to—but not exactly like—your brother or sister.

A dominant gene shows up most of the time. Brown eyes are dominant over blue eyes. A recessive gene shows up infrequently. Both blonde and red hair come from recessive genes. Dark hair is more common. If you look at the eye color and hair color of the people around you in class, you will see that this is true.

Genes help to make you who you are, but they don't tell the whole story. Your genes may help you to be fast, tall, or good-looking. But you still need to learn how to do things that you were not born with, such as being able to read or swim.

Check Your Understanding

1. A recessive gene
   a. shows up in most children.
   b. does not show up in most children.
   c. cannot show up in children.
   d. will not be passed on by the parents.

2. **Characteristics** means
   a. traits.
   b. dominant genes.
   c. recessive genes.
   d. codes.

3. One of Bailey's grandparents has green eyes. All of the others have brown eyes. Both of Bailey's parents have brown eyes. We can tell that Bailey's eyes are *probably*
   a. recessive.
   b. green.
   c. dominant.
   d. brown.

4. Juan has a brother. They look a lot alike because
   a. they have none of the same genes.
   b. they have many of the same genes.
   c. they have the exact same genes.
   d. one is adopted.

/4

Warm-Up

Name _____

2   Bird Migration

Birds that live where it gets cold in winter migrate. This means they fly south. As the days grow shorter in the fall, these birds shed their feathers. Their bodies react to the length of daylight. Losing feathers is called *molting*, and it takes energy. That is why birds are so much quieter in August and September than in the spring. Their energy goes toward molting instead of singing. With fewer feathers, the birds are lighter in weight, which helps them on the long flight south.

Why do birds migrate? It is a huge effort to fly hundreds of miles south, and then in the spring, to fly back again. Why don't they just stay where it's warm year round? The answer is food. In the spring and summer months, the North has more food. Many insects lay eggs in the fall that hatch the next spring. This means that birds that eat insects have little or no food supply in the winter, so they must go south.

Then, in the spring, the bugs in the North hatch. Birds have their babies in spring. Baby birds demand food all the time. Bugs are full of protein, and a high-protein diet helps the baby birds to grow their first feathers. So even those birds that do not eat insects themselves will feed them to their young.

Check Your Understanding

1. Eating bugs helps baby birds to
   a. grow feathers.
   b. learn to sing.
   c. learn to fly.
   d. hide from predators.

2. It is early March in the South. What will happen sometime this month?
   a. The Northern birds will fly north.
   b. The Southern birds will fly north.
   c. The Northern birds will fly south.
   d. The Southern birds will lay their eggs in the North and then fly home.

3. Birds molt in order to
   a. find a mate.
   b. find bugs to feed their babies.
   c. weigh less before a long flight.
   d. build a nest.

4. Northern birds that eat seeds and berries migrate. Why?
   a. They need to eat bugs during the winter.
   b. They cannot find enough food because it may be beneath snow and ice.
   c. They cannot find a mate if they don't migrate.
   d. They don't know how to build nests.

/4

Name _____

Toads

The toads you might see in your yard didn't start life there. In fact, they didn't even start out with legs. They hatched from eggs in a pond. They were tadpoles for ten days. They were much darker and smaller than frog tadpoles. Like fish, tadpoles have gills for breathing under water. As their limbs grow and their tails shrink, they develop lungs. Then, they hop out of the pond as tiny black toads no bigger than your little fingernail.

In the first summer, a toad grows so fast that it sheds its skin every three days. It develops the bumps on its skin during hibernation its first winter. These bumps fill with a fluid that makes the toad taste bad to some animals. If they catch a toad, they spit it out unharmed.

Toads catch bugs with their tongues and swallow them whole. Baby toads are the same size as many bugs. Yet no adult toad ever mistakes a baby toad for an insect. Toads can see a glow on another toad's skin, so they don't eat each other.

A toad can vomit. If it eats a toxic bug, the toad's stomach comes out of its mouth! It uses its right front paw to wipe its stomach. Then, the toad pulls its stomach back in using its strong throat muscles.

Check Your Understanding

1. When does a toad develop bumps on its skin?
   a. during the night
   b. during hibernation
   c. as soon as it stops being a tadpole
   d. the first summer of its life

2. Toad tadpoles breathe with their
   a. tails.   c. lungs.
   b. skin.   d. gills.

3. What color are toads when they first leave the pond?
   a. gray   c. black
   b. brown   d. green

4. Why do toads start life in a pond?
   a. A pond supplies their food and water while they develop.
   b. A pond is safer than land.
   c. A pond helps keep them clean.
   d. A pond gets more sunlight than land.

/4

Warm-Up

4   The Very Unusual Parrotfish

Name _____

All parrotfish are born female. They stay that way for about seven years. Then they turn into males! While they are females, they are dull red, brown, or gray. When they become males, they turn a bright green or blue with pink or yellow patches.

Parrotfish live on shallow coral reefs. They eat the colorful, hardened coral. How? They use their beak-like mouths to bite a chunk off the reef. Then, they crush it using teeth in their throats. This lets them get the algae in the coral. The fish's waste comes out as sand. This is one of the main ways that sand is made on a reef. (Sand also forms from erosion of the coral reef due to storms and wave action.)

Parrotfish want to stay safe while they sleep. So, the parrotfish secretes mucus from an organ on its head. It forms a bubble cocoon around itself. The cocoon hides the fish's scent. This means that the moray eel that hunts at night cannot find it. The cocoon helps the parrotfish in other ways, too. The mucus may repair damage to the fish's scales and gives some protection from harsh sunlight.

Parrotfish release many tiny eggs into the water. The eggs float. The ones that are not eaten sink onto the coral. They blend in and are not noticed until they hatch.

Check Your Understanding

1. Which is *not* a common way for sand to be made on a coral reef?
   a. storms
   b. waves
   c. fish digesting the coral
   d. boats striking the reef

2. What animal hunts for parrotfish?
   a. moray eel
   b. electric eel
   c. manta ray
   d. reef shark

3. How old are the oldest female parrotfish?
   a. 3 years
   b. 5 years
   c. 7 years
   d. 10 years

4. Why are female parrotfish a dull color?
   a. They eat dull-colored coral.
   b. They can hide in the reef's shadows.
   c. They blend in with the coral.
   d. They stand out against the sandy bottom.

/4

Name _____

Warm-Up 5   Common Bugs in Your Backyard

Two insects you may have seen are yellow jackets and ants. Both live in large groups. Yellow jackets live in gray paper hives. They are a kind of wasp. They are not afraid of people and might bother you at a picnic. They want your food. It is best to ignore them and not swat at them. If you do, you may end up running from an angry **horde**! When a yellow jacket is afraid, it gives off an odor. This tells other yellow jackets to help it. And, unlike a bee, a yellow jacket can sting over and over without dying.

There are 35,000 ant species. Ants have the largest insect brain. The combined number of brain cells in an ant colony equals the number of brain cells in one human! Ants are strong, too. They can lift up to 20 times their own body weight. Ants have six legs, and their jaws open sideways. They use their jaws to squeeze liquid from food. They will eat almost anything, from other insects to plants.

Ants have two stomachs. The first one is for its own food. The second one holds food it can spit out for other ants (babies or the queen). Each ant has two antennae that it uses to smell and touch. An ant works nonstop and can live to be 60 days old.

Check Your Understanding

1. How are yellow jackets and ants alike?
   a. They can lift 20 times their own body weight.
   b. They are very smart.
   c. They live alone and only seek each other out to mate.
   d. They live in colonies.

2. A synonym for **horde** is
   a. nest.
   b. ant.
   c. crowd.
   d. hive.

3. All ants have
   a. an odor they give off when frightened.
   b. two antennae and two stomachs.
   c. wings.
   d. gray paper hives.

4. How do yellow jackets differ from bees?
   a. They can sting many times without dying.
   b. They have a queen.
   c. They can fly.
   d. They live in hives.

/4

Warm-Up

6

Name _____

Head Lice

If you've ever had head lice, you know they are awful! The lice bite your scalp and suck your blood. This makes your head itch. Then, they lay up to 50 eggs on each strand of your hair each day! These eggs, or nits, are attached with special cement. It comes from the mother louse's body. Regular shampoo cannot break its bond. You must use anti-lice shampoo. If you don't kill the lice, the nits hatch in 8 to 10 days. They become adults in another 10 days and start laying eggs. Help!

Head lice cannot live more than two days without drinking human blood. They also cannot fly or jump. So how do they cause so much trouble? They move from an infected head to a new head. If a person with lice puts his head against the seat of an airplane and then you sit there next, you might get lice! Lice are so "catching" that if you have them, your school may make you stay home until your head is clear.

Each year, almost 10 million Americans get head lice. About 90 percent of those are children. That's because kids share things like hats, pillows, or sleeping bags with other kids. It's great to share, but some things are meant to be personal. You should never share your comb, hat, or hair ribbon.

Check Your Understanding

1. Head lice
   a. lay eggs on your skin.
   b. make your hair bleed.
   c. drink human blood.
   d. are not easy to catch.

2. Why do you need a special shampoo to get rid of lice?
   a. Regular shampoo does not suffocate the lice.
   b. Regular shampoo can't loosen the nits.
   c. Regular shampoo kills the nits but not the adult lice.
   d. Regular shampoo tastes good to head lice.

3. A boy caught head lice at a sleepover party. What probably happened?
   a. He shared a pillow with a kid who had head lice.
   b. He played a video game against a kid who had head lice.
   c. He drank from the same soda can as a kid who had head lice.
   d. He shared some food with a kid who had head lice.

4. Why are kids so apt to catch head lice?
   a. They don't shampoo often.
   b. They don't mind an itchy head.
   c. They refuse to get treated when they have head lice.
   d. They share things with others.

/4

Warm-Up
7

Name _____

Similarities Among Mammals

You are a mammal. Like all mammals, you are warm-blooded. You have hair. Your mother had milk for you to drink. Most mammals give birth to live babies, too. (Two Australian mammals lay eggs.) But did you know that you share bones with all mammals? Every mammal has one jawbone and three ear bones. All but two mammals have seven neck **vertebrae** (discs in the spine).

Scientists have found that mammals have similar bone structures. This is true even when they use the bones for very different purposes. Humans and bats have the same bones in their forelimbs. Of course we have arms and hands while bats have wings. You have one upper arm bone, two lower arm bones, and many wrist and hand bones. All of these bones are present within a bat's wings. Bats had a mouse-like ancestor. This animal had a bit of skin between its long, thin fingers. Over time the fingers grew longer. As a result, the flaps of skin between the fingers grew bigger. Gradually they became wings.

Our arm-bone structures are found in whales and dolphins, too. Their front flippers have bones that are very much like our arms and bats' wings. And, although whales and dolphins don't seem to have hair, they are born with it. It's on their faces! It soon falls out, and just the follicles remain.

Check Your Understanding

1. All mammals
  a. give birth to live babies.
  b. have one jawbone.
  c. have identical bones.
  d. have cold blood.

2. Vertebrae are the discs in your
  a. backbone.
  b. arm.
  c. wrist.
  d. fingers.

3. Which animal is *not* a mammal?
  a. a bat
  b. an elephant
  c. an eagle
  d. an opposum

4. The bones in your arm are similar to the bones in a
  a. dolphin's fin.
  b. cat's front leg.
  c. bat's wing.
  d. all of the above

/4

Warm-Up

8

Name _____

Heat

Heat moves from one thing to another by conduction. Some objects conduct heat quickly. Others do not. Suppose you take a hot pan from the oven. You use a potholder. The heat does not move from the pan through the cloth very fast. But, if you used a wet potholder, your hand might get burned. Why? Water conducts heat almost instantly.

Some materials do not conduct heat at all. Instead, the heat wrecks them. When exposed to heat, they melt or burn. Soft plastic melts; paper burns.

Metal conducts heat easily. Metal also expands when heated. This can cause a sun kink in a railroad track. In fact, a sun kink derailed an Amtrak train near the nation's capital in July 2002. It was a 100-degree day. The track's metal absorbed the sun's heat. This made the metal's atoms move. The hotter it got, the faster they moved. They hit nearby atoms and pushed them away. This made the track bend several inches. The train went off the tracks.

Since this accident, trains in the Washington, D.C. area do not run on hot days. However, scientists hope to design a fiber optic cable. It can be attached to the rails. It will ring an alarm when a sun kink starts to happen.

Check Your Understanding

1. How does heat move between items?
   a. by conduction
   b. by convection
   c. by electrical current
   d. by infusion

2. In the Amtrak derailment of July 2002, what happened second?
   a. The sun heated the metal rails.
   b. The track bent several inches.
   c. The train's wheels left the rails.
   d. The atoms in the rails moved rapidly.

3. Which of these objects conducts heat most rapidly?
   a. dry cloth
   b. metal
   c. paper
   d. wood

4. Heat always
   a. moves between items.
   b. destroys items.
   c. moves between items or destroys them.
   d. moves between items and then destroys them.

/4

Warm-Up 9

Name _____

Smart Animals

Scientists discovered a rat colony living on a **barren** island in the Pacific Ocean. There were no trees, plants, or grass. How had the rats managed to stay alive without food? Cameras were set up to watch the rats. Each rat sat on a rock and dangled its tail in the shallow water. Eventually a crab grabbed the "bait." Then the rat swung its tail up and around. It beached the crab and ate it.

Rats are highly intelligent. That's one reason why scientists spend so much time studying their brains.

Some birds are pretty smart, too. Green herons and crows can make and use tools. Scientists proved this with an experiment. First, they laid a few wires on the floor of a cage. Then they put one of these birds into the cage and added a chunk of fish. The bird couldn't reach the fish because it lay at the bottom of a long, thin tube.

The bird was frustrated because it wanted the food. Then it figured out what to do. It picked up one of the wires in its mouth and pressed it against the cage's bars to form a hook. Then it stuck the wire down the tube and pulled up the food! Before this experiment, scientists had believed that only primates could make and use tools.

Check Your Understanding

1. When the rats found themselves in a place without food, they taught themselves to
   a. swim.
   b. fish.
   c. beg from people.
   d. make a tool.

2. The word **barren** means
   a. bare, nothing there.
   b. full of life.
   c. distant.
   d. tropical.

3. Which animal cannot use a tool?
   a. a primate
   b. a crow
   c. a crab
   d. a green heron

4. The bird in the cage wanted to
   a. escape.
   b. hop from perch to perch.
   c. sing a song.
   d. eat the fish.

/4

**Warm-Up
10**

Name _____

Chelonians

Chelonians is the scientific name for tortoises and turtles. These reptiles have one thing in common: shells. Their spines are built into their shells. Most, but not all, can pull all their limbs and head inside it. Snapping turtles cannot pull their limbs or heads all the way in, though. They have very long necks—so long that if you pick one up by its shell, it can swing its head around and bite you!

Tortoises live on land in warm, dry places. They need to live where it's hot because they are cold-blooded. This means that their body temperature is the same as the air around them. They are too heavy to swim. They eat plants. They breathe with lungs.

Turtles are expert swimmers. They eat small fish, bugs, worms, and frogs. A few eat plants, as well. Turtles breathe with lungs. This means that they cannot stay underwater and never come up for air. Even so, a few turtle species can actually live for a week underwater without having to take a breath of air! How? They can take in oxygen from the water through their skin and the lining of their throats.

Some breeds of tortoises and turtles can live to be more than 100 years old. The growth rings on the shell help to show the animal's age.

Check Your Understanding

1. All chelonians
   a. have shells with spines.
   b. have the ability to pull in their heads and limbs.
   c. live on land and water.
   d. live mostly in water.

2. All chelonians breathe with their
   a. skin.   c. shells.
   b. gills.   d. lungs.

3. Which animal always eats plants?
   a. snapping turtle   c. tortoise
   b. turtle   d. the article does not say

4. Why shouldn't you pick up a snapping turtle by its shell?
   a. It can kick you really hard.
   b. It can swing its head around and bite you.
   c. Its shell will break in two if it's handled.
   d. It may hurt itself pulling its head and limbs all the way into its shell.

/4

Name _____

Warm-Up

11

Can You Hear That?

Humans can only hear some sounds. We cannot hear the high frequencies that dogs do. That is how hand-held dog repellers work. A person walks down the street. A snarling dog runs toward the person. The person presses a button on the dog repeller. It makes a high-frequency sound. The person cannot hear it. But the dog hates it! It runs away from the person.

Bats make ultra-high frequency sounds that we cannot hear. These sounds echo, or bounce off, bugs. The noise returns to the bat's ears. That's how bats find food in the dark. They hunt only at night. A bat can hear an insect's footsteps! This process is called *echolocation*.

Humans do not hear very low frequencies, either. Giraffes make low-frequency sounds. Some people, even those who work in zoos, thought that giraffes were silent. They never heard them make noise. But that is just because we do not hear their sounds. Why do they make low-frequency sounds? In the wild, giraffes live in herds. They roam the grassy plains in Africa. If a giraffe gets lost, it calls out to the herd. Its low-frequency sound will go farther than a high-frequency one. And the lions and cheetahs that want to eat it cannot hear its call. Whales, elephants, and rhinos use low-frequency calls, too.

Check Your Understanding

1. Which animal makes an ultra-high frequency sound?
   a. a giraffe
   b. a dog
   c. an elephant
   d. a bat

2. How does a dog repellent work?
   a. It gives a dog an electric shock.
   b. It makes a noise that the dog dislikes.
   c. It forms an invisible wall that only a dog can feel.
   d. It transmits a human voice staying, "Stop!" to a dog.

3. Which animal does not make a low-frequency sound?
   a. a whale
   b. a giraffe
   c. a cheetah
   d. a rhinoceros

4. Compared to humans, most dogs can hear
   a. higher frequencies than humans can.
   b. lower frequencies than humans can.
   c. none of the same frequencies that humans can.
   d. fewer sounds than humans.

/4

Warm-Up

12 Salmon

Name _____

Most fish can only live in fresh water *or* saltwater. Salmon live in both. After they are born in fresh water, their bodies go through several big changes. At the same time, they swim down the river toward the sea. In their final change, they go through smoltification. This lets them live in saltwater. Then they swim out into the ocean.

In the ocean, salmon grow rapidly, reaching up to 50 pounds. Killer whales, sharks, harbor seals, and sea lions eat them. If they can avoid predators, the fish spend up to four years at sea before returning to their own birthplace.

How do they know the way? Some scientists believe they "smell" their way back to where they hatched. They swim upstream against strong currents. When they reach the right place, the female makes a nest. She pumps her tail to make a dent in the gravel of a streambed. Her action attracts a male. After she lays her eggs, the male covers them with sperm. Then the female pumps her tail again. She covers her nest with gravel. She does this several times. There are thousands of eggs in each nest.

All salmon die within a month of mating. Their bodies fill the stream and provide food for birds and bears.

Check Your Understanding

1. Most fish
   a. live their lives in whatever kind of water they hatch in.
   b. can live in either fresh or saltwater.
   c. live half their lives in fresh water and half their lives in saltwater.
   d. can only live in brackish water (mixture of fresh and saltwater).

2. How do male salmon find eggs to fertilize?
   a. They go through smoltification.
   b. They can smell the eggs.
   c. They pick mates in the ocean and then follow the females all the way upstream.
   d. They are attracted by the female's actions of making the nest.

3. Salmon are most closely related to
   a. dolphins.
   b. frogs.
   c. rainbow trout.
   d. turtles.

4. Salmon swim against the current so that they
   a. return to their birthplace to lay eggs.
   b. get plenty of exercise.
   c. cannot be found by predators.
   d. can find a large food supply.

/4

Warm-Up

13   Our Moon Came From Earth

Name _____

No one is 100 percent sure how Earth's moon formed. However, most scientists think that it is a chunk of Earth. How did it get up there? More than four billion years ago, a large meteor hit Earth. It may have been the size of Mars! Luckily, it did not hit Earth head-on. If it had, our planet would have been destroyed. It hit Earth at a glancing blow.

The heat from the impact made the rock that broke off so hot it was fluid. These huge chunks of molten rock flew into space. Earth's gravity made these chunks begin to orbit. Over many years, the pieces drew together to form the moon. They cooled down. Now our moon is a just a big, cold rock. Its surface is marked with big holes made by all the meteors that have struck it.

Both Earth and the moon have a solid core of iron and nickel in the center. Both have a mantle of semi-melted rock and a cool, hard crust. The magma inside Earth often spills from volcanoes onto its crust. The moon has not had a volcano erupt in 150 million years. Its magma is much cooler than Earth's. It rarely makes it onto the surface.

Check Your Understanding

1. Both Earth and its moon
    a. have the same temperature magma.   c. have a solid core.
    b. have frequent volcanic eruptions.   d. are the size of Mars.

2. The moon probably formed
    a. from pieces of Earth.
    b. from meteors drawing together into a single mass.
    c. from space dust.
    d. at the same time as Earth.

3. The moon does not have any
    a. nickel on it.   c. iron on it.
    b. magma on it.   d. plants on it.

4. Why does the moon have big holes on its surface?
    a. Long ago, Earth bumped into it and caused the holes.
    b. It has been hit by meteors.
    c. Satellites keep running into it.
    d. Volcanic eruptions have caused the holes.

/4

Warm-Up

14   Escaping From Predators

Name _____

All animals have a survival instinct. This means they want to live. No animal wants to be eaten by another. So animals have ways to stay safe. The horned lizard is a reptile. It lives in the American Southwest. If it sees an animal that wants to eat it, the horned lizard will stay very still. The lizard's skin color blends in with the ground. This helps it to be less visible. If the predator does spy him, the lizard will gulp air. He will fill his lungs. In this way, he swells up and looks big and puffy. This lizard also has horns that make it look like it might harm an attacker. Some of the animals that see the lizard will decide that it would not be a good meal. If an animal still wants to eat it, the lizard will shoot blood from the corners of its eyes! By squeezing its blood vessels, the lizard can aim the spray. It can shoot five feet through the air.

Salamanders are amphibians. They have a way to escape snakes. When a snake grabs one with its mouth, the salamander will secrete mucus. It is a gooey fluid. It is thick and sticky. The salamander fills the snake's mouth with mucus. The mucus makes it so that the snake can't close its mouth. The salamander wriggles free! Over time, the mucus dissolves. The snake looks for something else to eat.

Check Your Understanding

1. Salamanders are a type of
   a. lizard.
   b. mammal.
   c. amphibian.
   d. snake.

2. Which animal shoots blood from its eyes to protect itself?
   a. a salamander
   b. a snake
   c. an eagle
   d. a horned lizard

3. Which is most like mucus?
   a. hair gel
   b. lemonade
   c. sand
   d. ice cream

4. The salamander must use its defense
   a. before the snake ever opens its mouth.
   b. before the snake grabs the salamander.
   c. before the snake swallows the salamander.
   d. after the snake has closed its mouth.

/4

Warm-Up
15

Name _____

Wind Patterns

You know that a dry day can turn wet if wind brings in a rainstorm. A cool day will heat up if wind blows from a warmer area. But do you know what causes the wind to blow? The sun! In fact, the sun causes most of Earth's weather.

The sun heats Earth's surface and its atmosphere. But they do not heat evenly. The air above Earth's hot areas rises into the atmosphere. Air from a colder area flows in to replace the heated air. This air movement, or circulation, causes winds to form over large parts of Earth. These prevailing winds differ with latitude. Over the equator, heated air rises fast. Cooler air rushes in to replace it. This forms the trade winds. The trade winds do not blow straight toward the equator. Due to Earth's rotation, they blow at an angle. In the days when ships moved by sails, sailors used these trade winds to guide their ships.

However, near the equator and for about 700 miles on either side of it, there are no prevailing winds. Sailors hated this calm region. They called it the *doldrums*. No wind would fill the sails. They would get stuck there. They had to wait for their ship to drift into a sea current or an area that had wind.

Check Your Understanding

1. What is the air movement around the globe called?
   a. doldrums
   b. trade winds
   c. circulation
   d. latitude

2. Look at paragraph 2 again. You can tell that hot air always
   a. rises.
   b. sinks.
   c. brings rain.
   d. brings dry weather.

3. The trade winds
   a. blow along the equator.
   b. are unpredictable.
   c. blow straight toward the equator.
   d. are on both sides of the doldrums.

4. Around the world, prevailing winds differ based on the
   a. equator.
   b. latitude.
   c. longitude.
   d. moon.

/4

Name _____

Earthworms Improve Soil

Have you ever seen earthworms on a road or sidewalk after it rains? First, rain soaked into the ground. The earthworms live underground. They could not breathe. So they wriggled up to the surface. Some flowed with the rain onto the hard surface of the road. If they don't get back to the soil, they will die. Why? Earthworms need dirt. It is not only where they live but also what they eat.

Earthworms can tunnel through dirt at the amazing rate of 10 inches per minute. Their entire bodies are made of muscles. They use them to wriggle. They eat the dirt as they go. They get energy from bacteria and rotting roots and leaves. They eat one-third of their body weight each day. They pass the rest as waste called *casts*.

Earthworms are helpful. Their movements bring air into the dirt. And their casts make the soil more fertile for growing things. Earthworm casts are five times richer in nitrogen, seven times richer in phosphates, and eleven times richer in potash than the surrounding dirt. This means worm casts are one of the best fertilizers. Some people buy earthworms to add to their gardens. In a farmer's field, there may be one million earthworms eating ten tons of dirt each year in one acre of soil.

Check Your Understanding

1. What is an earthworm's waste called?
   a. potash
   b. phosphate
   c. nitrogen
   d. casts

2. How do earthworms improve the soil in which they live?
   a. They remove air from the soil.
   b. Their casts contain nutrients that plants need.
   c. They increase the bacteria in the soil.
   d. They keep the soil moist.

3. What part of the dirt is actually providing food for the worms?
   a. bacteria
   b. dead leaves
   c. rotting plants
   d. all of the above

4. If earthworms do not surface when it rains, they will
   a. drown.
   b. have no food to eat.
   c. be more obvious to birds.
   d. have better nests.

/4

Warm-Up

17

Name _____

Rabbits

You have probably seen different rabbits. There are 48 breeds. Some, like the Flemish giant, are huge. Others, like the Netherland Dwarf, are small. Some rabbits have short hair. Some have long hair. There are even lionhead rabbits. Their fur is short everywhere except around their head. It looks like a lion's mane. Rabbits come in all shapes, sizes, and colors. Have you ever wondered why?

People bred rabbits based on the traits they liked best. These traits could be things like size, color, or fur. People bred these rabbits together in the hopes that the babies, or kits, would have the good traits. Over time, this selective breeding created new breeds.

Rabbits don't all look alike, but they mostly act alike. None of them eat meat. They all hop, chew, and eat hay or grass. Yet tame and wild rabbits are different. In fact, tame and wild rabbits cannot have kits together. The reason is that they have a different number of chromosomes. Tame rabbits have 22. Wild rabbits have 21. Jackrabbits (hares) have 24.

All tame rabbits came from wild European rabbits. They lived in **warrens**, which are tunnels under the ground. The wild rabbits in North America always live above the ground.

Check Your Understanding

1. What does a lionhead rabbit look like?
   a. It has short fur.
   b. It has long fur.
   c. It has no fur.
   d. It has short fur with long fur around its head.

2. A **warren** is a
   a. rabbit cage.
   b. rabbit's underground home.
   c. baby rabbit
   d. kind of rabbit.

3. Rabbits were first domesticated (tamed) in
   a. Europe.
   b. North America.
   c. Asia.
   d. Africa.

4. Why can't tame and wild rabbits produce kits?
   a. They have different color fur.
   b. They are different sizes.
   c. They have different chromosomes.
   d. They eat different things.

/4

Warm-Up

18

Name _____

Don't Spread Germs!

Germs are what make you sick. They can move from dirty hands to food when a person does not wash his or her hands before making or eating food. Germs move from raw meat to a person's hands. If the person doesn't wash and touches the salad, the greens now have the germs. When the meat is cooked, the germs will die. But since the salad is not cooked, the germs remain.

Germs can move from a sick person to a healthy one if a person wipes his nose and then touches something. Then another person picks the item up and gets the germs. That's why washing your hands when you are sick is really important.

The germs that cause colds, and eye, ear, and throat pain can move from a sick person to a well one through hand contact, too. Always wash your hands after touching the part of you that feels ill (such as rubbing eyes).

Germs can also spread through the air. The best way to stop that is to cover every cough and sneeze with a tissue or by using the inside of your elbow. Then wash your hands. Because dirty hands spread most germs, wash your hands with soap and water often. Get rid of the germs before they get into you!

Check Your Understanding

1. How does washing your hands help you?
   a. It washes away the germs that can cause illness.
   b. It makes you well when you're already sick.
   c. It makes germs get smaller.
   d. It changes germs so that they can't make you sick.

2. Germs can spread
   a. through the air.
   b. by touch.
   c. in food.
   d. all of the above.

3. Which of these events happens last?
   a. You make a sandwich without washing your hands first.
   b. You get sick.
   c. You eat the sandwich.
   d. The germs on your hands end up in the sandwich.

4. If people washed their hands more often every day,
   a. people would stop getting sick.
   b. there wouldn't be enough soap.
   c. there would be fewer germs that spread.
   d. there would be better-tasting salads.

/4

Warm-Up 19

Name _____

Unusual Mother Animals

When you think about mother animals that take care of their young, you picture birds and mammals. Most reptiles and amphibians lay eggs and go away. They expect the eggs to hatch, and they don't do anything to help their offspring. In the same way, most insects lay their eggs and leave. The eggs hatch, and the young must take care of themselves. That's why the mother shield bug is so unusual. First, she glues her eggs to her mate's back. He carries them around until they hatch. After they are born, the mother shield bug guards them from harm.

The jungle scorpion is unusual, too. She gives birth to about 30 live young. As they are born, she grasps them with her front claws and helps them onto her back. Then she walks around with her babies on her back for two weeks. She gets them food until they are ready to let go and find their own.

Female aphids give birth to live young. For an insect, that's really rare. Once she has given birth, the aphid leaves the babies on their own. Most of them are quickly eaten by other bugs and birds. It's a good thing they are tasty. One aphid can produce one billion aphids in six months! Without their predators, we'd be overrun by aphids.

Check Your Understanding

1. Female aphids are unusual because they
   a. glue their eggs to their mate's back.
   b. help predators to find their babies.
   c. give birth to live young.
   d. take care of their offspring.

2. Jungle scorpions
   a. glue their eggs to their mate's back.
   b. give birth to live young and then leave.
   c. lay eggs.
   d. take care of their offspring.

3. How many aphids can a single aphid produce in a year?
   a. one million aphids
   b. two million aphids
   c. one billion aphids
   d. two billion aphids

4. Which animal would you expect to take care of its young?
   a. a hawk
   b. a lizard
   c. a mosquito
   d. a frog

/4

Warm-Up

20

Name _____

Ospreys, Expert Fishers

Like eagles and hawks, ospreys are birds of prey. They live on every continent except for Antarctica. An adult weighs about 3.5 pounds and has a wingspan of five feet. When they are about three years old, ospreys pick a mate for life. They build huge nests high above the ground. Some have even built nests atop telephone poles. A nest can weigh 400 pounds! The birds line their nests with soft grass and reuse them each year. The nests are always close to where the parents fish.

Each spring, females lay three or four eggs. The fluffy white chicks want food constantly. The parents hunt nonstop to meet their demands. The first chick to hatch will always be the strongest. The parents always feed it first. In years when food is **scarce**, it may be the only one to live. Within eight weeks, the chicks can fly. Young ospreys have orange eyes. When they get old enough to mate, their eyes turn brown. This lets other ospreys know that they are adults.

Ospreys fold their wings close to their bodies and dive into the water feet first. They go completely underwater to get a fish. They have a special nasal passage to keep water from entering their noses. Water slides off their dense, oily feathers. An osprey's footpads have tiny sandpaper-like barbs to hold wriggling, slippery fish.

Check Your Understanding

1. Which is not a bird of prey?
   a. a hawk
   b. a robin
   c. an eagle
   d. an osprey

2. The word **scarce** means
   a. unusual.
   b. usual.
   c. not plentiful.
   d. plentiful.

3. How can ospreys tell the difference between a young bird and an adult bird?
   a. by feather length
   b. by feather color
   c. by size
   d. by eye color

4. Why do osprey parents always feed the chicks in the order in which they hatched?
   a. to be sure that at least one survives
   b. to keep track of who is who
   c. to make it fair for the chicks
   d. to make sure they all survive

/4

Warm-Up 21

Name _____

Meteors

Have you ever seen a shooting star? It wasn't a star. It was a falling meteor. It shot across the sky. Then it faded fast. Since most meteors do not contain metal, they burn up. They never make it to the ground.

Each November, Earth passes through a part of space filled with gas, dust, and rocks left behind by a comet. The result is a **spectacular** meteor shower. You can see it at night without a telescope. But if the sky has clouds, you'll miss it.

Meteors are space rocks. Millions enter our atmosphere each day. Almost none reach the ground. Very rarely, those that hit the ground leave big holes. Arizona has a huge dent in the ground called Meteor Crater. A meteor that fell 50,000 years ago made it. About 25,000 years ago, a meteor crashed in Texas. It left a hole 175 yards wide. That is almost the length of two football fields! Over time, dirt and rocks filled in the hole. Now, most people don't even know it is there. In both cases, the meteor fell apart when it hit.

In 2009, a meteor shot across the Texas sky. Small pieces of it were found in a field. In 2010, a meteor caused a loud boom. It fell in Wisconsin. Both were small meteors. They did not make craters.

Check Your Understanding

1. In order to see a meteor shower, you need a
   a. cloudless night sky.
   b. cloudy night sky.
   c. telescope.
   d. set of special glasses.

2. A synonym for **spectacular** is
   a. dull.
   b. daytime.
   c. impressive.
   d. nighttime.

3. In order to leave a crater, a meteor must
   a. be small.
   b. be large.
   c. make a loud noise.
   d. not contain any metal.

4. You look at the night sky and see a small flash of light. It lasts a few seconds and then vanishes. You just saw a
   a. falling star.
   b. meteor burn up.
   c. jet plane.
   d. communications satellite.

/4

Warm-Up
22

Name _____

Clever Animal Traps

Lions, tigers, and wolves are hunters. They see animals they want to eat and run after them. If they catch them, they have a feast. Many smaller carnivores don't have the brute strength and speed to catch their meals. Yet they do have clever ways to catch their prey. A praying mantis hides among leaves. It blends in so well, it is almost **invisible**. It stays very still with its forelegs ready to strike. When a bug goes past, the praying mantis lunges, grabs the bug, and quickly chews it up.

You know that spiders spin webs. Then they wait for flies to get stuck in the web. But the Portia spider of Australia does something else. It taps on the web of another spider. When the spider rushes over to get the "fly," the Portia eats it instead.

The trapdoor spider digs a hole just big enough for itself. It uses silk and dirt to form a trapdoor above its head. When an ant steps on the door, the spider grabs it. Using a similar ploy, the ant lion larva buries itself in the ground. Its mouth is aimed at the sky. When an ant runs over its mouth, it falls right in! And because ants follow each other's trails, often many ants fall in.

Check Your Understanding

1. A praying mantis
   a. blends in with its surroundings.
   b. eat plants.
   c. can outrun its prey.
   d. captures bugs in flight.

2. The antonym of **invisible** is
   a. wiggly.   c. quiet
   b. noisy   d. visible.

3. Both the trapdoor spider and the ant lion larva create traps for
   a. flies.   c. ants.
   b. spiders.   d. small rodents.

4. The Portia spider tricks its prey by making the prey think that the Portia spider is
   a. another spider.   c. an ant.
   b. a fly.   d. larvae.

/4

Warm-Up
23

Name _____

Earthquakes

Our Earth's crust is like an eggshell. The shell has cracks. The cracks are between huge pieces of rock. They are called *tectonic plates*. Below Earth's crust is another layer. It is melted rock. It is thick like pudding. The big plates float on it. They bump into each other. One plate may slip past the other. This can cause an earthquake. Then the ground shakes. Buildings may fall down. Large cracks may open in the ground.

Scientists measure the movement. They find out the quake's **magnitude**. The more the ground shakes, the higher the magnitude. People have kept records. So far the strongest earthquake had a 9.5 magnitude. It was in Chile. It is a nation in South America. That quake occurred in May 1960. It was bad. But it wasn't the worst in terms of lives lost. The deadliest earthquake was in 1556. It was in China. About 830,000 people died. Another deadly quake struck in 2004. It happened under the sea. It caused big waves. They hit Southeast Asia. More than 229,000 people died.

In March 1964, the strongest earthquake ever to strike North America hit Alaska. It had a 9.2 magnitude. The quake damaged the city of Anchorage. In some places, the soil changed to a liquid form. This fluid state just lasted three minutes. But during that time, many buildings fell down. And a chunk of downtown slid into the sea!

Check Your Understanding

1. A tectonic plate is
   a. an underwater earthquake.
   b. Earth's melted rock layer.
   c. a huge piece of Earth's crust.
   d. a crack between the pieces of Earth's crust.

2. The word **magnitude** means
   a. location.
   b. cause.
   c. danger.
   d. strength.

3. Which of these earthquakes happened third?
   a. a 9.2-magnitude quake in North America
   b. a 9.5-magnitude quake in South America
   c. an undersea earthquake in Southeast Asia
   d. a quake in Asia that killed 830,000 people

4. During the earthquake in Alaska, what unusual condition occurred?
   a. The ground shook.
   b. The dirt became liquid.
   c. Cracks opened in the ground.
   d. Tectonic plates bumped or slid against each other.

/4

Warm-Up

24

Name _____

The Great Pacific Garbage Patch

Have you ever heard of the Great Pacific Garbage Patch? It is a place in the sea where a large amount of trash circles in a current. This mass of debris is twice the size of Texas! It has been growing for more than 50 years. The garbage is 80 percent plastic and weighs about 3.5 million tons. The most common kind of trash floating there is plastic shopping bags. How did they get there? Water flows downhill until it reaches the sea. Plastic bags that fall to the ground often end up in water that ends up in the ocean.

To make matters worse, ocean animals mistake pieces of plastic for food. They fill their stomachs with it. They can't digest the plastic. The animals slowly starve to death. Yet no one knows how to clean up the mess. The only thing we can do is to keep it from getting bigger.

About 380 billion plastic bags are thrown away each year in the United States. Some of those bags will end up in the Great Pacific Garbage Patch. What can you do? Stop using plastic bags! When you get just one or two items in a store, say, "I don't need a bag." If you do have your items bagged, use reusable bags or be sure to recycle the plastic bags.

Check Your Understanding

1. The Great Pacific Garbage Patch began forming when people
   a. reached the West Coast.
   b. redirected the currents in the Pacific Ocean.
   c. began using paper bags.
   d. began using plastic bags.

2. Eight out of every ten items floating in the Great Pacific Garbage Patch are made of
   a. rubber.
   b. plastic.
   c. wood.
   d. leather.

3. You get a plastic bag from the store. What is the best sequence of events?
   a. Take it home, empty it, and throw it into the trash.
   b. Take it home, empty it, and throw it on the ground.
   c. Take it home, empty it, and burn it in a woodstove.
   d. Take it home, empty it, and put it in a recycling bin.

4. What might you see near the Great Pacific Garbage Patch?
   a. a sea turtle with a plastic six-pack ring around its neck
   b. people swimming around plastic bags
   c. flies buzzing around trash
   d. commercial fishing boats

/4

Warm-Up

25   Gray Whales, Amazing Travelers

Name _____

Gray whales are huge. Adults grow up to be the length of a bus! They can weigh 20 to 40 tons. Females are larger and heavier. Gray whales take a long time to grow up, too. A female can first have a baby when she is eight years old. These whales can reach the age of 60.

The gray whales spend their summers in waters off Alaska. They spend the winters near Baja, California. That's where the females give birth and raise their babies. A female has a baby every other year. She carries the calf for 13 months. At birth, a calf is 15 feet long and weighs 2,000 pounds! (Proportionally, if a human baby were this big at birth, he would be born two feet tall and weigh 50 pounds!)

The whale baby nurses for seven months. The calf must grow a layer of blubber. It needs warmth for the annual migration. Each year these whales migrate 10,000 miles up and down the cold waters of the Pacific coast. They swim 5,000 miles each way. They have the second-longest migration of any animal. In 40 years of migrating, a gray whale swims the distance to the moon and back!

Check Your Understanding

1. Baby gray whales drink their mother's milk for
   a. 3 months.
   b. 5 months.
   c. 7 months.
   d. 13 months.

2. A gray whale can live to be
   a. 8 years old.
   b. 20 years old.
   c. 40 years old.
   d. 60 years old.

3. Which event happens second in a female gray whale's life?
   a. She has a calf.
   b. She makes her first journey to Alaska.
   c. She makes her first journey to California.
   d. She drinks milk from her mother.

4. In which body of water would you expect to find a gray whale?
   a. the Pacific Ocean
   b. the Indian Ocean
   c. the Southern Ocean
   d. the Atlantic Ocean

/4

Name _____

Warm-Up

26   **Smart Stoplights**

People must take turns on the road so everyone gets where they are going safely. That's why stoplights control intersections. When both roads are very busy, the light has a timer. First, the cars on one road get to move for half a minute. Then, the cars on the intersecting road get to move for half a minute.

Some stoplights are at the **junction** of a busy road and a less-busy road. These stoplights only make the cars on the busy road stop if a car is waiting on the less-busy road. But how does a stoplight know that a car is waiting? Under the road lies a piece of iron with large coils of wire wrapped around it. It acts like a magnet. This device is located in the pavement at a point before cars reach their stopping point. It is placed when the road is built or repaved. A car engine has lots of metal in it. As the car engine passes over the wire coil, the magnet senses it. The magnet triggers the stoplight to change.

First, the light changes to yellow and then red. This makes the cars on the busy road slow down and then stop. Then, the light changes to green for the waiting car. Some intersections have a small laser. As a car drives past, it blocks the laser. This tells the stoplight that a car is waiting.

Check Your Understanding

1. At the busiest intersections, stoplights
   a. use a device to detect when a car is waiting.   c. use laser beams to detect traffic.
   b. are put on a timer.   d. are not used.

2. The word **junction** describes a
   a. place where two roads meet.
   b. device that detects cars waiting at an intersection.
   c. smart stoplight.
   d. laser used at a busy intersection.

3. Road designers bury a large magnet under the road to
   a. count the number of cars that use the road.
   b. let the stoplight operate without electricity.
   c. make the stoplight change because a car is waiting.
   d. keep the pavement from buckling on hot summer days.

4. When a stoplight is yellow, it means
   a. the light is about to change to green.   c. stop.
   b. stop and then go.   d. the light is about to change to red.

/4

Name _____

27   Reduce Your Carbon Footprint!

Global warming is changing our planet. There is too much carbon dioxide being put into the air. Carbon dioxide is a greenhouse gas. It holds heat close to Earth. Your carbon footprint is how much carbon dioxide you put into the air through your actions. Everyone needs to reduce his or her carbon footprint. That includes you.

There are lots of ways to reduce your carbon footprint. One of the easiest ways is to recycle everything that you can. Melting down an aluminum can to make a new can takes much less energy than mining aluminum and creating a can from scratch. There's no limit to the number of times an aluminum can may be recycled.

Return plastic bags to the store. Take cloth bags to the store. You can use them again and again.

Use less energy. Always turn off the lights when you leave an empty room. Do not leave your computer on overnight. Don't keep your house too cool in the summer and too warm in the winter. It takes energy to run an air conditioner or a furnace. Dry your clothes on a line instead of using a clothes dryer. Cook in a microwave instead of heating the whole oven. Do not use paper or plastic cups, plates, and utensils. They take a lot of energy to make. Then they take up space in a landfill as waste.

Check Your Understanding

1. Your carbon footprint is a measure of how much carbon dioxide
   a. you breathe out each day.
   b. you breathe in each day.
   c. is released by your behaviors.
   d. gets absorbed by the oceans.

2. How does recycling reduce carbon dioxide in the atmosphere?
   a. It takes less plastic to recycle an item than to make a new one.
   b. It takes less energy to recycle an item than to make a new one.
   c. It takes less metal to recycle a can than to make a new one.
   d. It takes less time to recycle an item than to make a new one.

3. You reduce the amount of carbon dioxide entering the air when you
   a. keep your house warm in summer and cool in winter.
   b. keep your house cold in summer and hot in winter.
   c. use your oven instead of your microwave.
   d. leave your computer on overnight.

4. One way to reduce your carbon footprint is to
   a. vacuum your room.
   b. make your bed.
   c. stop doing laundry.
   d. let dishes air dry instead of using the dishwasher's heat cycle.

/4

Warm-Up 28

Name _____

Disrupting Ecosystems

Sometimes people get rid of a species. This is always bad news. Why? It wrecks food webs. Food webs need prey and predators. The people in Malawi, Africa, found this out the hard way. Leopards had killed some cattle and dogs. The government said the farmers could kill any leopard they saw. So they did. But then there were no leopards left to eat the baboons. Soon there were too many baboons. They ate the people's crops. They caused worse problems than the leopards had!

Sometimes people get rid of a whole ecosystem. This causes trouble, too. Wetlands give homes to a wide variety of wildlife. They also provide drainage for miles around. Before they knew this, people filled in many of these damp, low-lying areas. Then they built farms, homes, and cities. But when wetlands are drained, mosquitoes breed out of control. At first scientists couldn't figure out why. Then they realized that rain puddles gave the mosquitoes places to lay eggs. Yet the puddles could not provide homes for the ducks that eat the mosquitoes. So, scientists restored a 1,500-acre wetland. In a short time, the number of mosquitoes fell by 90 percent!

Check Your Understanding

1. A natural predator for mosquitoes is a
   a. duck.
   b. baboon.
   c. leopard.
   d. skunk.

2. Why did an overpopulation of baboons cause big problems?
   a. They killed too many leopards.
   b. They ate the crops that people needed for food.
   c. They killed people's cattle and dogs.
   d. They attacked people.

3. How did restoring the wetland make the mosquito population drop?
   a. It caused a fatal disease to spread through the mosquito population.
   b. It removed the places where mosquitoes breed.
   c. It brought back the mosquitoes' predators.
   d. It abruptly changed the life cycle of mosquitoes.

4. What do you think they did in Africa to control the baboon population?
   a. They used insecticides.
   b. They restored a wetland.
   c. They restored a whole jungle.
   d. They reintroduced a few leopards.

/4

Warm-Up
29

Name _____

Robots

Have you seen the movie *Wall-E*? It makes robots seem almost human. But robots are not like us. That's why they are better at certain things. Most robots do dull tasks that people don't like to do. They do such jobs faster and without mistakes. Let's say a robot fastens a screw on each item on an assembly line. The robot does not get bored. It does not get sick. It does not go on vacation. A robot can work in places that are too dangerous for a human, too. For instance, robots can fix pipes deep underwater. The water pressure is too high for humans down there.

Robots that have sensors can do more. Sensors on the robot take readings. Then, the robot's computer program makes a choice. For example, a robot's job may be to pick up something breakable. The sensors keep the robot from holding it too tightly. They keep the robot from dropping the item, too.

Robotics is the science of making robots. In addition to the typical robots, scientists have made some complex ones. They cost a lot more because they can move around. They have electronic sensors. They may carry cameras. They operate based on a mix of stored instructions, sensor feedback, and remote control. These robots have gone where no human has ever been. Some have been on Mars. Others have gone to the deep sea floor.

Check Your Understanding

1. Which job might a robot do?
   a. discuss different cake choices with the customer
   b. stir cake batter
   c. write names and sayings in frosting on cakes
   d. taste-test the cake

2. A robot's sensors
   a. allow it to think for itself.
   b. helps the robot to do the same task over and over and over.
   c. keep it from making mistakes.
   d. make it cost less than a robot without sensors.

3. The majority of robots
   a. do dull jobs.
   b. have been to Mars.
   c. are smarter than humans.
   d. operate underwater.

4. The people who design robots work in the field of
   a. robotists.
   b. robotics.
   c. robotology.
   d. robotron.

/4

Warm-Up
30

Name _____

Deep-Sea Discoveries

There's only one sure thing about science: We don't know everything. The coelacanth is a fish that lives off the coast of Africa. It lives in deep water. It rarely comes near the surface. The only fossils of it are millions of years old. Scientists were sure that this fish went extinct even before the dinosaurs died out. Then, a fisherman caught a coelacanth in 1938. The man knew it was unlike anything he had ever seen. He contacted scientists. When they examined it, they were shocked. Since then, just a few more of these fish have been captured. The most recent was in 1998.

The frilled shark is another "extinct" fish that turned out to be alive. The first living one was caught in Japan in 2007. It was filmed. However, it died quickly. So far no others have been found.

No one thought the giant cranch squid was extinct. They thought it was just a scary story. Then, in 2003, the first photos were taken of a live 30-foot-long squid. It lives in the deep waters off Antarctica. It weighed half a ton. Its eyes were the size of volleyballs! In 2007, a complete corpse of one was found.

What else may lurk in the sea that we don't know about? Only time will tell.

Check Your Understanding

1. Before 2003, scientists thought that the giant cranch squid was
   a. extinct.
   b. not real.
   c. green.
   d. rare.

2. In what year was the first coelacanth found?
   a. 1938
   b. 1998
   c. 2003
   d. 2007

3. The frilled shark was filmed
   a. off the coast of Antarctica.
   b. off the coast of Africa.
   c. in the waters off Japan.
   d. in the waters off Jamaica.

4. How did the animals in this article escape notice for so long?
   a. Scientists were not interested in them.
   b. Scientists have no way of comparing new species to known species.
   c. These animals only come near the sea's surface in winter.
   d. These animals very rarely come near the sea's surface.

/4

From the Past

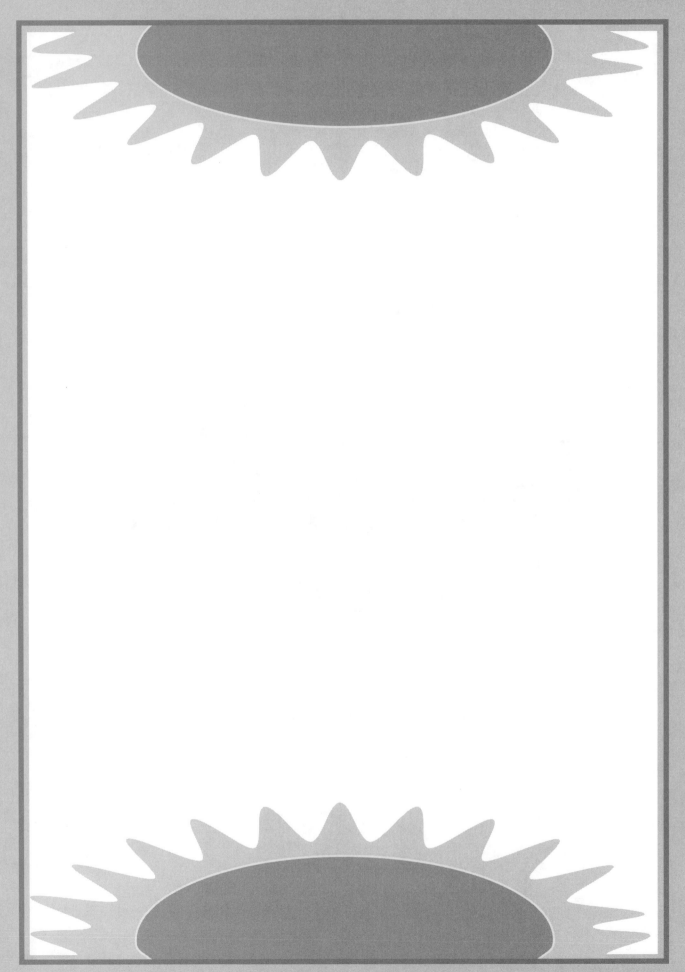

Name _____

Tasty Discoveries

It was early March long ago. A Native American named Woksis lived in what is now New York State. One night, he stuck his hatchet in a maple tree. It was near the longhouse where he lived. The next day, he grabbed the hatchet. He went hunting. Soon his wife saw something flowing from the cut in the tree. She put a bucket below the drip. She liked the idea of getting water from the tree. It would save her a walk to the creek.

That night she boiled meat for dinner. She used the "tree water." Her family loved the taste of their meal. She had gathered maple sap. When she boiled it, it turned into maple syrup. Now, each year, the United States makes more than one million gallons of maple syrup. Canada makes five million gallons a year.

Tea is a popular drink all over the globe. The only thing that people drink more of each day is water. Tea was discovered in 2737 BCE. Shen Nung was boiling water outdoors in China. Wind blew leaves from a bush into his open kettle. Shen Nung removed the leaves. Then, he tasted the solution. It was great! He had others try it, too. Almost everyone liked it. And that's still true. Last year, people drank more than 855 billion cups of tea.

Check Your Understanding

1. How many gallons of maple syrup does Canada produce each year?
   a. 1,000,000
   b. 2,700,000
   c. 5,000,000
   d. 10,000,000

2. Each day, what do people drink the most of?
   a. water
   b. maple syrup
   c. coffee
   d. tea

3. Both Woksis's wife and Shen Nung
   a. invented new foods on purpose.
   b. discovered something delicious by accident.
   c. became rich and famous from their discoveries.
   d. marketed their products to people around the world.

4. Why do you think Woksis and his family liked the meat boiled in tree water?
   a. It was spicy.
   b. It was salty.
   c. It was sour.
   d. It was sweet.

/4

Name _____

Warm-Up 2 — From Trees to Ships

Before 1865, all ships were wooden. The lumber came from tall, straight white pines. This way, the boards were long enough to make ship frames. The ships were built in towns by the sea. Soon the town ran out of nearby trees. They had to get lumber from another place.

New Hampshire and Wisconsin had huge forests of white pine. Loggers did the dangerous work of cutting these trees. They used axes to chop down the trees. They lived in forest camps.

These forests were far from railroads or big rivers. So the loggers used oxen and horses to drag the trees to small rivers. For much of the year, the rivers were too shallow to carry the logs. But in March, when all the snow melted, these rivers would be deep enough to carry all those logs.

All year long, the loggers piled the logs beside the river. When March came, they'd push the logs onto the frozen river and wait for it to thaw. The sudden melting of all the snow and ice would carry the logs away. Daring men balanced on the floating logs to guide them downstream. The logs would float to a sawmill. The sawmill used large spinning blades to split the logs. Once the logs were sliced into boards, shipbuilders could use them.

Check Your Understanding

1. Loggers cut down the trees with
   a. axes.
   b. hand saws.
   c. circular saws.
   d. chain saws.

2. At the start of what month did loggers push the stacked logs onto the river?
   a. January
   b. March
   c. July
   d. December

3. White pine lumber is good for shipbuilding because these tall trees
   a. are insect resistant.
   b. are easy to climb.
   c. can float down rivers.
   d. grow straight.

4. What happened at the sawmill?
   a. The trees were cut down.
   b. The logs were stacked by a river.
   c. The trees' needles were removed.
   d. The logs were made into boards.

/4

Warm-Up
3

Name _____

True Lighthouse Tales

Most of the time, tending the light in a lighthouse during the 1800s was dull. You couldn't leave. The light had to glow day and night. Otherwise, ships could run aground. Yet, when it wasn't dull, storms could make the job scary.

Matinicus Rock Light stands on an island 18 miles off the coast of Maine. In 1856, Sam Burgess was its light keeper. He rowed to the mainland to buy food for his family. As he stepped into the rowboat, he told his 14-year-old daughter Abbie that she was in charge. His wife was ill. Abbie was the oldest of the four children. A gigantic storm kept him from returning for

a whole month. When he got back, he found that Abbie had kept the light burning. She had also taken good care of her mother and sisters.

In 1870, a huge storm struck Hendricks Head Light in Southport, Maine. Winds drove a ship onto the rocks. It sank with all the people on the ship. At dawn, the light keeper looked for survivors. He heard a cry. It came from a box with two mattresses tied to it. Inside were a baby and a note that said that she was the captain's daughter. He was "putting her into God's hands." The keeper and his wife raised the child as their own.

Check Your Understanding

1. A light keeper did not get time off from his job because
   a. constant storms prevented him from leaving.
   b. the light had to be kept lit at all times.
   c. he needed to save people on a daily basis.
   d. he had to give tours to important people who stopped by.

2. What was Sam Burgess most likely worried about while he was on the mainland for a month?
   a. if his family had run out of food
   b. if all the members of his family were ill
   c. if a ship had run into the lighthouse
   d. if one of his daughters had fallen into the ocean

3. Why didn't the lighthouse prevent the 1870 shipwreck at Hendricks Head?
   a. The storm was so bad that the crew on the ship couldn't see the light.
   b. Waves wrecked the lighthouse.
   c. The light keeper had forgotten to light it that night.
   d. The ship was pushed by high winds.

4. The sea captain tied mattresses to the box because he
   a. believed they would make the box more obvious in the water.
   b. thought they would help provide air inside the box.
   c. hoped they would help the box float to shore.
   d. wanted the baby to have the mattresses as she grew up.

/4

Warm-Up

4

Name _____

Shipwrecked in Antarctica

Ernest Shackleton wanted to be the first to travel across Antarctica. In 1914, he and his crew of 27 set out on the ship *Endurance*. When their ship was 100 miles from Antarctica's shore, ice closed around it. The ship was stuck for 10 months. Then the ice started to crush its hull. The men packed all the supplies they could carry in three rowboats. The men walked on the ice dragging these boats through freezing winds. Each night they slept in sleeping bags on the ice.

Sometimes sea leopards followed the men's shadows through the ice. They burst through cracks in the ice with their jaws opened wide. The men hunted and ate them. They caught fish, too.

At last, the men made it to Elephant Island. Most of the crew stayed there. Shackleton and five men set out in a small boat. They rowed for 800 miles through stormy seas. As soon as they landed on South Georgia Island, the captain got a ship. He went back for his men. But the seas were rough. It took him three months to get close to Elephant Island.

The waiting men saw sails coming toward them. They were saved! Every man had survived one of the biggest adventures of all time.

Check Your Understanding

1. Shackleton and five men set out in a rowboat to go to
   a. South Georgia Island.
   b. Antarctica.
   c. Endurance.
   d. Elephant Island.

2. Which was *not* a danger faced by the men after they left the ship?
   a. falling through the ice
   b. being eaten by an elephant
   c. being eaten by a sea leopard
   d. freezing to death

3. How did the men get to Elephant Island?
   a. They walked there while dragging boats.
   b. They rode on the backs of sea leopards.
   c. They sailed there in the ship.
   d. They rowed there in rowboats.

4. Why were the men better off on Elephant Island than they had been on the ice floes?
   a. It was much warmer on Elephant Island.
   b. They could find more things to eat.
   c. They were on land and therefore wouldn't fall through the ice.
   d. They were more likely to be seen by a passing ship.

/4

Warm-Up

5   The Discovery of Pompeii

Name _____

Pompeii was an ancient city. It lay at the base of Mount Vesuvius. This volcano erupted in 79 CE. First, the mountain sent out a spray of red-hot rocks and pebbles. They rained down on the city. Next, it sent out a cloud of toxic gases. This killed all living things. Then, it spewed ash. Tons of it fell. It covered the city like a blanket. The ash was 12 feet deep. It formed an airtight seal. For over 1,500 years, the city lay buried. Since oxygen did not reach the area, things did not rot.

Within 100 years, people forgot about Pompeii. Then, in 1595, a worker dug a tunnel. He found a part of the buried city. No one cared. In 1748, a man from Spain began to dig in the ruins. He found that the paint of the wall murals was bright. Jugs held wine that tasted good! He also found people. A soldier stood at his post. Another man stood with a sword in one hand and his foot atop a chest. It held gold and silver coins. He probably wanted to keep it from the five men lying nearby. The bodies were actually shells. Scientists poured plaster into the shells. They made copies of the dead. One can see the expressions on their faces! About 2,000 bodies have been found.

Check Your Understanding

1. Vesuvius is the name of the
   a. ancient city.
   b. volcano.
   c. man who dug in the ruins.
   d. worker who dug a tunnel.

2. When were the first jugs of wine uncovered at Pompeii?
   a. 1595
   b. 1712
   c. 1748
   d. 2000

3. Why hadn't the ancient things rotted?
   a. Ash kept oxygen from reaching the bodies.
   b. Red hot ash killed all life, including bacteria.
   c. The toxic gases preserved everything.
   d. People had hidden their belongings in cedar chests.

4. Why do you think no one seemed to care about the first discovery of Pompeii?
   a. People thought the tunnel digger was just kidding.
   b. The tunnel digger did not tell anyone.
   c. Scientists did not realize it was an important discovery.
   d. The tunnel digger told people but then quickly covered it up again.

/4

Name _____

6   World War II Submarines

Japan attacked Pearl Harbor. It sank a lot of U.S. ships. So America entered World War II. Japan is an island nation in the Pacific Ocean. All of its fuel came by ship. So did all the materials needed to build planes, ships, and submarines.

The Americans did not want the Japanese to get fuel or supplies. So U.S. submarines were sent to sink the ships carrying goods to Japan. These subs did an amazing job. They caused more than half of Japan's shipping losses.

U.S. subs rescued American pilots who had their planes shot down over the sea, too. The first President George Bush was a Navy pilot. He was saved by a sub.

Life on a submarine was tough. The air was stuffy. It was crowded. There was no place to be alone. In the main aisle of the sub, each man had to pause while someone squeezed past. Each bunk was barely big enough to lie down. Serving on a sub was scary, too. If an enemy found a sub, the sailors had to shut down its engines. Then they had to hope that the depth charges fired on them would miss.

Many men on the subs lost their lives. More than 3,600 of them lie in watery graves where their subs went down.

Check Your Understanding

1. The Japanese needed supply ships because
   a. the ships were so reliable and always delivered all of the goods.
   b. they didn't have the money to develop their resources.
   c. it was cheap to import fuel.
   d. they didn't have the supplies on their own islands.

2. On a historical time line, what happened second?
   a. U.S. subs picked up downed American pilots.
   b. U.S. subs attacked supply ships.
   c. The Japanese lost World War II.
   d. The Japanese attacked Pearl Harbor.

3. Why are so many submariners on the bottom of the ocean instead of in a cemetery?
   a. Their families didn't want their bodies returned to them.
   b. They asked to be buried at sea.
   c. It was too difficult to find them and bring them back to the surface.
   d. People in wars aren't buried; their bodies are left lying wherever they die.

4. Picture a World War II submarine far below the water. How can the captain see what is happening on the surface?
   a. only by bringing the submarine up to the surface
   b. by opening a hatch
   c. by having some men swim to the surface
   d. by using a periscope

/4

Warm-Up

7 Women Spies in the American Revolution

Did you know that women spies helped to win the American Revolution? George Washington led the American troops. His men were up against the world's strongest army. He knew that he had to outsmart them. And it worked. Major George Beckwith led the British spies. At the end of the war, he said, "Washington didn't outfight us. He out-spied us."

The American spy ring was called the Culper Gang. This group of men and women acted as if they were loyal to the British. The British spoke in front of them. Then, the spies sent information to Washington. Anna Smith Strong lived in what is now New York State. The British held the area. Still, she found a way to send information to Washington. When she hung a black petticoat (slip) on her clothesline, it meant she had facts. The number of hankies she hung told where the facts would be found. She hid notes under a rock and in a hole in a tree. The British never caught on.

Lydia Darragh owned a tavern. She heard the British plans. Then, she wrote on tiny notes. She sewed them under cloth-covered buttons. She sewed the buttons on her son's coat. The boy walked to the American camp. Washington cut off his buttons. Then, Washington let false battle plans fall into British hands. They moved troops to the wrong place.

Check Your Understanding

1. How did Lydia Darragh find out about British war plans?
   a. She listened to them talk in her tavern.
   b. She listened from behind a tree.
   c. She received notes from them underneath buttons.
   d. She figured out the code they used with hankies on a clothesline.

2. What color petticoat did Anna Smith Strong hang when she had facts to share?
   a. white
   b. pink
   c. brown
   d. black

3. Who was the head of the British spies?
   a. George Washington
   b. George Beckwith
   c. George Culper
   d. George Darragh

4. Washington wanted the British to have false battle plans so that they would not
   a. have enough troops in the correct location.
   b. have their own spies.
   c. have enough supplies.
   d. discover the members of the Culper Gang.

/4

Warm-Up
8   Surnames

Name _____

Your parents chose your first and middle names. They gave you their last name, too. But where did that **surname** come from? All surnames have meanings. Many of the meanings have been lost over time.

During the 1800s, many people left Europe. They moved to the United States. These people had lived in tiny towns. There, everyone called a man named Karl by his first name. If there was more than one Karl, people called them Karl, Neil's son or Karl, Robert's son. A daughter was called Ann, John's daughter.

When these people came to the United States, they had to think of a last name on the spot in order to become a citizen! As they entered the port, an official asked for their names. If a man said he was Jack's son, his last name was written down as Jackson. A woman who said she was from the town of Wahl was given the last name of Walton.

Some people based their names on their job. This explains the surnames of Baker, Miller, Tailor, or Gardener. Others ended up with Blacksmith or Goldsmith. Smith is a shorter form of these names.

Check Your Understanding

1. Which sentence in the text told you the main idea?
   a. Some people based their names on their jobs.
   b. All surnames have meanings.
   c. Your parents chose your first and middle names.
   d. As they entered the port, an official asked for their names.

2. A **surname** is a
   a. first name.
   b. middle name.
   c. last name.
   d. nickname.

3. In the 1800s, a person entered the United States without a surname. He made furniture in his home nation. The official probably gave him the surname
   a. Carpenter.
   b. Miner.
   c. Miller.
   d. Forest.

4. A person who has the surname Butler probably had an ancestor who
   a. tended gardens.
   b. was a coal miner.
   c. took care of sheep.
   d. worked as a servant.

/4

Warm-Up 9

Name _____

Horses Helped Humans

Long ago, horses were wild animals. They lived in Europe and Asia. Then people got the idea to tame them. Horses are smart. They can be trained. They are strong, too. Horses are strong enough for a person to ride. They can pull heavy loads. Horses can move much faster than a person can. So hunters on horses could catch more animals. They brought home more food. Horses also helped to win wars. Soldiers fought on horseback. The people without horses would often lose.

There were no horses in America 600 years ago. Then explorers came. They brought horses with them on ships. Some of these horses ran away. They formed herds of wild horses. The Native Americans saw these new animals. They saw that they were fast and strong. They decided to catch them and train them. After that, the Native Americans rode horses, too.

For thousands of years, horses were the best way to move on land. They were the fastest, too. But horses are not often used for **transportation** today. In most places, cars, buses, and trains are the best ways to travel on land.

Now people mostly ride horses for sport and fun. Some horses do work. Ranchers ride horses to round up cattle. Police horses carry officers through the streets of some cities. Horses pull people in carriages, sleighs, and hay wagons, too.

Check Your Understanding

1. Which event occurred first?
   a. Horses came over in ships.
   b. People in Europe and Asia tamed horses.
   c. Some horses ran away.
   d. The Native Americans had horses.

2. **Transportation** means
   a. moving people and things from one place to another.
   b. selling things in a store.
   c. going on a vacation.
   d. any motor vehicle, like a car, train, or plane.

3. Today, horses are no longer ridden for
   a. fun.   c. cattle ranches.
   b. sport.   d. battles.

4. Picture the ships that first brought horses to America. What kind were they?
   a. speed boats   c. wooden with sails
   b. steamships   d. rowboats

/4

Warm-Up
10

Name _____

Making Glass

People have made glass for thousands of years. Glass is made of sand (75 percent), soda ash (15 percent), and lime (10 percent). These ingredients are mixed together. Then, they are heated to 2,400°F in a furnace. All glass was hand-blown. A man stuck a long iron rod into a blob of hot, molten glass. Then he blew into the rod to create a bottle. He would blow the glass like you blow through a straw. As the glass was cooling, he would swing it back and forth to lengthen the bottle. Often, hand-blown bottles had little air bubbles in them.

The glass press was invented in 1826. It let liquid glass be poured into molds. When the glass hardened, it took the shape of the mold. Glass items like dishes and bottles were mass-produced for the first time. It had cost one cent to make a hand-blown glass bottle. Fifteen machine-mold bottles could be made for one cent!

Windows were still hand-blown. First, men blew the glass into eight-foot-long tubes. While these tubes were still hot, they were sliced down one side, put back into a furnace, and then rolled flat. The glass sheets cooled. Then they were cut to measure, packed in straw in wooden boxes, and sent by rail to stores. In 1924, a machine could roll window glass flat. No blowing was needed.

Check Your Understanding

1. Glass is a melted mixture of
   a. sand, lime, and soda.
   b. lime, sand, and ash.
   c. ash, salt, and lime.
   d. soda ash, sand, and lime.

2. Which event occurred second?
   a. The glass press was invented.
   b. Everything made of glass was hand-blown.
   c. Windows were mass-produced.
   d. The cost of making bottles dropped.

3. About how much time passed between when bottles and windows were hand-blown and when they could be mass-produced?
   a. 40 years
   b. 60 years
   c. 80 years
   d. 100 years

4. You can tell that hand-blown glass windows
   a. did not take much skill to make.
   b. were rolled flat in the first step.
   c. may have had little air bubbles in them.
   d. did not cost very much money.

/4

Warm-Up

11

Name _____

A Whale of a Tale

Whales were once hunted for their blubber (fat). When heated, their blubber turns into oil. Before electric lights, most lamps used whale oil. The oil was also used to make soap, leather, candles, and makeup. Some kinds of whales were hunted close to extinction.

Today, right whales are endangered. Their name comes from whale hunters who said that they were the "right" ones to kill. They swam slower than other whales. They usually swam close to the coast. They floated when dead. They had a large amount of blubber. One whale could produce as much as 7,000 gallons of oil. In the 1600s, they were the first whales hunted as a business. They were hunted for nearly 300 years.

For the past 60 years, a law has protected right whales. Yet there are less than 350 of them left in the North Atlantic Ocean. Why? Ship propellers hit them. Many get tangled up in fishing nets. Because whales are mammals, they breathe with lungs. They drown when they get trapped underwater.

The Center for Coastal Studies tries to save the whales. One whale, named 2030, had three fishing ropes wrapped around her body. Rescuers cut two of the three ropes. They put a tracking device on the whale. But just a month later, she died from the wounds from the third rope.

Check Your Understanding

1. About how many gallons of oil can one right whale produce?
   a. 1,600
   b. 3,000
   c. 2,030
   d. 7,000

2. Whale oil was used to make
   a. gasoline.
   b. candles.
   c. ropes.
   d. electricity.

3. About how many years have right whales been protected?
   a. 60
   b. 300
   c. 350
   d. 1,600

4. Why do rescuers try to save whales?
   a. They get paid for each whale they save.
   b. They want to be rich and famous.
   c. They don't want the whales to become extinct.
   d. They don't want dead whales to wash ashore in tourist areas.

/4

Name _____

Warm-Up 12

The Dead Sea Scrolls

Did you know that a boy made one of the best archaeological finds of all time? He found the Dead Sea Scrolls in 1947. The boy had gone in search of his lost goat. He saw a small opening in the side of a cliff. He threw a stone inside to see if the goat was in there. He heard something break. He wondered if treasure lay inside the cave. Two days later the boy squeezed through the narrow slit. He saw several large stone jars. They held two very old parchment scrolls. The scrolls were wrapped in linen and leather. The boy took them down the mountain. He showed them to people in town. An archbishop in Jerusalem bought them.

Scholars looked at these scrolls. They had them carbon dated. The scrolls were about 2,100 years old. This made them 1,000 years older than any other Bible texts. The Dead Sea Scrolls made front-page news around the world.

The people living in the area rushed to look for more scrolls. In 1952, they found more. They were less than a mile from the first site. Soon, pieces of 400 scrolls with parts of nearly every book of the Old Testament had been retrieved. Archaeologists know that an ancient group of Jewish monks lived in the area. No one is sure why they wrote the scrolls and then hid them.

Check Your Understanding

1. A boy found the Dead Sea Scrolls when he was looking for
   a. his sister during a game of hide and seek.
   b. things to sell to American collectors.
   c. hidden treasure.
   d. a missing goat.

2. What is the main idea of this passage?
   a. A boy discovered a cave and squeezed inside.
   b. The Dead Sea Scrolls made front-page news around the world.
   c. Jars hidden in caves held ancient scrolls containing parts of the Bible.
   d. An archbishop in Jerusalem paid the boy for old parchment scrolls.

3. Which event occurred last?
   a. Scholars read the scrolls.
   b. A boy found a cave.
   c. Monks hid jars in the cliffs.
   d. Monks wrote scrolls.

4. The second set of scrolls was discovered around
   a. 60 years ago.
   b. 95 years ago.
   c. 105 years ago.
   d. 150 years ago.

 /4

Name _____

The Story of the Stars and Stripes

The United States became a nation in 1781. It had fought a war to be free of Great Britain's control. Yet the new nation chose the same colors for its new flag. They were red, white, and blue. The flag had 13 stripes. The seven red stripes stood for bravery. The six white stripes stood for purity. The flag also had 13 white stars. They were on a blue background. There was one star for each of the 13 colonies. These colonies had joined together to form the new nation. These colonies became the first states.

As more states joined the union, the United States grew bigger. By 1795, there were 15 states. So, the flag changed. It had 15 stars and 15 stripes. By 1817, there were 20 states. The flag changed again. This time it had 20 stars and 20 stripes.

People disliked the new flag. They said there were too many stripes. The flag looked crowded. So in 1818, a law passed. It said that the flag would always have 13 stripes and one star per state.

Today the American flag has 13 stripes and 50 stars. The last state was Hawaii, added in 1959. Since then, the American flag has had 50 white stars on a blue background.

Check Your Understanding

1. The seven red stripes are a symbol of
   a. bravery.
   b. freedom.
   c. purity.
   d. the number of original colonies.

2. Why was a flag law passed in 1818?
   a. to keep the flag's colors red, white, and blue
   b. to keep the flag from getting too many stripes
   c. to add stripes to the flag
   d. to limit the number of states that could join the Union

3. If Puerto Rico was made a state,
   a. it would have no effect on the U.S. flag.
   b. another stripe would be added to the U.S. flag.
   c. another star would be added to the U.S. flag.
   d. another star and another stripe would be added to the U.S. flag.

4. You can tell that the state of Hawaii
   a. did not change the U.S. flag.
   b. wanted to change the number of stripes on the U.S. flag.
   c. had no effect on the U.S. flag.
   d. was the 50th one to join the Union.

/4

Warm-Up
14

Name _____

Mysterious Disappearances at Sea

In December 1872, a British ship was sailing in the Atlantic Ocean when its crew saw another ship. It didn't look right. The sails were missing. Nobody was at the wheel. The ship just rocked in the water.

The captain took some men and rowed over to the *Mary Celeste*. The ship seemed fine. It had no leaks. The barrels it carried as cargo were still lashed in place. The galley held plenty of fresh food and water. There were no signs of struggle. But there was no one on board. Two lifeboats were gone, too. The last entry in the captain's log was dated two weeks before. Based on his notes, the ship had drifted hundreds of miles. None of the *Mary Celeste's* crew was ever found. No one knows what happened to them.

In 1955, another abandoned ship made headlines. The *Joyita* was drifting in the South Pacific Ocean. It was partially flooded. All its lifeboats were gone. The radio was sending a distress signal. But it was useless. The antenna was broken. An engine fire had occurred. There were bloody bandages, too. The 25 people aboard were never found. One theory is that the captain died. The people panicked. They got into the lifeboats. They left the ship. Yet they never made it to shore.

Check Your Understanding

1. The name of the rescue ship in 1872 was
   a. the *Mary Celeste*.
   b. the *British*.
   c. the *Joyita*.
   d. not given.

2. What was wrong with the *Mary Celeste*?
   a. It was sinking fast.
   b. Its entire crew was missing.
   c. It had been on fire.
   d. It was the scene of a bloody battle.

3. What do we know for sure about the *Joyita*?
   a. The captain died.
   b. Several people bled to death.
   c. A fire destroyed most of the ship.
   d. There was an engine fire.

4. You can conclude that the people aboard the *Mary Celeste* and the *Joyita*
   a. got into the lifeboats.
   b. deliberately drowned themselves.
   c. were washed off their ships by huge waves.
   d. were hurt and thrown overboard.

/4

Name _____

Warm-Up 15

Ancient Egyptian Mummies

The ancient Egyptians thought that dead people needed their bodies after death. They believed in an afterlife. So, they found a way to keep dead bodies from rotting. They turned the dead people into mummies. Ordinary people were not turned into mummies. But all the kings and queens were **preserved** this way.

Making a mummy took a lot of work. First, priests washed the body. Then, they removed all of the organs. They even pulled out the brain—through the nose! They put a kind of salt all over the body. After six weeks, the body dried out. Next, they stuffed the body with sand, sawdust, or cloth. This made the body look full again. Then, they rubbed spices and oils into the skin. Finally, the priests wrapped cloth strips tightly around each body part. Wrapping the body took about two weeks. They laid the body in a coffin. The coffin's cover had paintings and sometimes gems. The coffin was put in a tomb.

The most famous mummy is King Tut. He was a teenager when he died. This was over 4,000 years ago. He was laid in a secret tomb. Scientists found it in 1922. King Tut's mummy lay inside a solid gold coffin. His family had put gold, gems, and other riches into his tomb. Even his sandals were made of gold.

Check Your Understanding

1. Ancient Egyptians believed dead kings and queens
   a. would use their belongings after they died.
   b. should be burned instead of buried.
   c. would send good luck to their people.
   d. would return to their throne after they died.

2. What did the priests do last when making a mummy?
   a. They washed the body.
   b. They removed the organs.
   c. They wrapped the body.
   d. They stuffed the body.

3. Egyptians mummified their rulers because they
   a. thought it would make the rulers look better in the afterlife.
   b. thought the rulers needed their bodies in the afterlife.
   c. wanted to use the rulers' organs.
   d. hoped the rulers would be found years later.

4. An antonym of **preserved** is
   a. kept.
   b. worshipped.
   c. ruined.
   d. changed.

/4

Warm-Up

16

Qin's Amazing Clay Army

Name _____

In 1974, some farmers dug a well. It was near Xi'an, a city in northern China. They uncovered something surprising. Buried in the ground were several lifelike clay heads! The men took the heads home. Archaeologists came to study them. They started digging in the same place. What they found amazed the world.

They uncovered a huge pit. It had a brick floor. It had a roof of pine logs. Inside stood 8,000 life-size soldiers. They were made of baked clay. There were horse statues, too.

Each soldier in the army can be told apart from all the others! Their heads were made from one of 12 molds. But eyes, noses, and hair were carved by hand. Each one has a **unique** look. Armor and arm and leg positions add variety, too. Each figure has a bronze sword or spear. The army guards Emperor Qin's tomb. He lived from 259 to 210 BCE. He was the first Chinese emperor. He came to power at the age of 13. He told craftsmen to make a clay army to serve him in the afterlife. It took the workers 37 years to create it.

People built a museum over the pit to protect the figures. It is one of the world's most popular tourist sites.

Check Your Understanding

1. Qin Shi Huangdi was the
   a. last Chinese emperor.
   b. first Chinese emperor.
   c. name of the place where the emperor's terracotta army was found.
   d. name of the emperor's palace.

2. The soldiers and horses are made of
   a. wood.
   b. bronze.
   c. clay.
   d. glass.

3. You can tell that the emperor
   a. believed that there was an afterlife.
   b. thought that his tomb was too big.
   c. enjoyed riding horses.
   d. wasn't proud of his army.

4. An antonym for **unique** is
   a. antique.
   b. handcrafted.
   c. unusual.
   d. identical.

 /4

Name _____

Ghost Towns

What is a ghost town? It's a place where people once lived and worked. Now no one lives there. All that is left are buildings and the echoes of a time long ago when the streets bustled with people.

Most ghost towns began as boomtowns in places where gold or silver was found. Many people rushed there to find some. This happened several times in U.S. history. The first was the California Gold Rush. There were gold rushes in Colorado, South Dakota, and Alaska, too. Each time people heard there was gold to be found, they raced there. All the miners needed food, places to live, and services. So some people went to the town to open boarding houses and general stores. They set up laundries and tailor shops. Often the service providers made the most money. Why? The miners needed to eat and have a place to sleep, whether they found any gold or not.

With so many people looking for it, all of the natural resource was found quickly. The gold (or silver) ran out. People saw there was no more money to be made. When the miners left, there was no need for lodging or other services. So the owners of those places left, too.

Check Your Understanding

1. Most ghost towns
   a. had their population abruptly disappear and no one knows why.
   b. are haunted by spirits.
   c. had a population that grew slowly.
   d. were originally boomtowns.

2. Which event would most likely have occurred third?
   a. Silver was discovered in Colorado.
   b. The amount of silver was not enough to support the town.
   c. Miners rushed to Colorado to get the silver.
   d. People built a mining town in Colorado with stores, restaurants, and hotels.

3. The person most likely to get rich in a mining boomtown
   a. owned the general store.
   b. worked as a farmer.
   c. worked as a miner.
   d. provided entertainment.

4. Which natural resource is *not* mined?
   a. gold
   b. diamonds
   c. lumber
   d. coal

/4

Warm-Up
18   The Story of the Statue of Liberty

Did you know that the Statue of Liberty came from France? The French people gave it as a gift for America's 100th birthday in 1876. But it took years to build her. In 1884, she was completed. Then she was too big to send! It was taken apart and packed in 214 boxes. The boxes were loaded onto a ship. The trip took weeks. At one point, the ship nearly sank in a big storm. But eventually the statue arrived in the U.S. It was 1885.

Once it arrived, the statue needed a base to stand upon. There was no money to build one. A New York newspaper had a way to help. They offered to print the name of every person who gave money for the base. People sent money. Finally, the base was built. It measures at 154 feet in height.

At last Miss Liberty was put back together. It took four months. She stands proudly on Liberty Island in New York City. One hand is raised. In it, she holds a torch. In the other hand, she holds a tablet. Written on the tablet is a date. The date is July 4, 1776. This date is Independence Day for the United States. The statue is 151 feet tall. The whole thing measures 305 feet from the ground to the tip of her torch. The Statue of Liberty was dedicated in front of thousands of people on October 28, 1886.

1. What might be one reason the Statue of

Check Your Understanding

Liberty was not shipped in one piece?
   a. It was so big.
   b. It was made in France.
   c. The boat was too crowded.
   d. The base was made in the United States.

2. You can conclude that
   a. the French were angry at the U.S.
   b. nobody liked France's birthday gift to the U.S.
   c. people liked having their names printed in the newspaper.
   d. the statue was an easy project to put together.

3. What would probably have happened if the ship carrying the boxes had sunk?
   a. People would have dove down and brought up the pieces of the statue.
   b. Miss Liberty might still be in pieces on the bottom of the ocean.
   c. Miss Liberty would be standing on Liberty Island just as she is today.
   d. The French would have been happy.

4. In what year was America "born"?
   a. 1676
   b. 1876
   c. 1976
   d. 1776

/4

Name _____

The Legend of John Henry

In the early 1870s, men were making the Big Bend Tunnel. It is on the Chesapeake and Ohio Railroad in West Virginia. To make the tunnel, the men used long-handled hammers to pound a steel drill into the rock. They took the drill out and stuffed the hole with blasting powder. Then, they blasted away the rock inside the mountain.

John Henry was a strong African-American worker. His strength amazed those who met him. One day, a man brought his newly invented steam drill to the site. He said that 20 workers swinging hammers couldn't make a hole as fast. He wanted the foreman to buy it. The workers were afraid. They thought the machine would take their jobs.

John Henry swore that he could beat the steam drill in a race. A famous song says that John Henry won the race. But he had worked so hard that he had a heart attack and died. The fact is that John Henry did beat the steam drill. But it did not kill him. He died later. A large rock fell from the tunnel's ceiling. It crushed him.

The song about him was written in 1900. It has kept his memory alive. John Henry was an important symbol to workers at a time when they feared that machines would replace them.

Check Your Understanding

1. What was John Henry's job at the Big Bend Tunnel?
   a. to dig the tunnel by chipping away at it with a hammer
   b. to make holes for blasting powder
   c. to sing so the men would swing their hammers at the same time
   d. to lay railroad tracks in the tunnel

2. Which event occurred third in John Henry's life?
   a. People wrote a song about him.   c. He won a race with a machine.
   b. He said he would beat the steam drill.   d. He was hired to work on a railroad tunnel.

3. How did John Henry die?
   a. He died in his sleep.   c. He had a heart attack on the job.
   b. He was crushed on the job.   d. He died of old age.

4. Why did workers want to keep John Henry's memory alive?
   a. He showed that workers are better than machinery.
   b. When the steam drill killed him, it proved that machines were evil.
   c. He died a hero while saving his fellow workers from disaster.
   d. He wrecked the steam drill so it wouldn't take away anyone's job.

/4

Warm-Up
20   Changing the World, One Page at a Time

Name _____

Long ago, every book was copied by hand using a quill pen. A quill pen was a bird feather dipped in ink. It took years for one monk to make one copy of a book. He spent his life copying the same book. This made books cost so much that only the rich could afford them. Few people knew how to read. With few books and readers, ideas and knowledge spread slowly.

Then, in 1450, Johannes Gutenberg invented movable type and the printing press. He made hundreds of pieces of metal "type." There were pieces for each punctuation mark, number, and letter. He used these letters to form words in rows in a tray. Next, he rolled ink on the tray. Then, he pressed paper against it. This moved the ink onto the paper. He hung the page on a clothesline to dry. Later, a man sewed the pages in order with heavy thread. He put a fabric cover on the book.

Gutenberg's invention let ideas and knowledge spread faster and easier than ever before. The printing press made books cost less, too. More people had books. More learned how to read. By 1900, knowing how to read was the rule rather than the exception in Europe.

Check Your Understanding

1. What did the monks do once they finished copying a book?
   a. They started to make another copy.
   b. They died because they'd finished their goal.
   c. They quit being monks and became farmers.
   d. They learned to read.

2. Gutenberg invented the printing press about
   a. 250 years ago.
   b. 550 years ago.
   c. 850 years ago.
   d. 1,000 years ago.

3. The invention of the printing press is somewhat like the invention of the
   a. cell phone.
   b. copy machine.
   c. wheel.
   d. clothes dryer.

4. The printing press changed how people shared ideas. Which of these inventions has had as great an impact?
   a. the typewriter
   b. the fax machine
   c. the Internet
   d. the cell phone

/4

Name _____

Colossal Statues

The word *colossal* means huge. It comes from the Colossus of Rhodes. It was a statue of Helios, the Greek sun god. The bronze statue had a raised torch. It guarded the harbor of Rhodes, a Greek island. Built in 280 BCE, it was 160 feet tall. Its size was meant to scare away attackers. The metal to make it came from the melted weapons of fallen enemies. But the gigantic statue stood just 54 years. It fell during an earthquake in 226 BCE. It lay in ruins for nearly 1,000 years. Then its pieces were sold. Not even a trace of it remains.

Since 1931, a colossal statue has stood atop a mountain in Brazil. It is called the Christ the Redeemer statue. It is 125 feet tall. Its arms are open wide in a 98-foot span. The statue is large. Its position on a mountain peak makes it seem gigantic. It towers above the city of Rio de Janeiro.

The Motherland Monument is a woman with a sword raised in the air. She honors those who fought the Battle of Stalingrad. It was part of World War II. The statue stands in Russia. It was built in 1967. It is 270 feet tall. It weighs more than four tons.

Check Your Understanding

1. Which statue is/was the tallest?
   a. Helios
   b. Motherland Monument
   c. Christ the Redeemer
   d. Colossus of Rhodes

2. Which statue has been standing for more than 75 years?
   a. Christ the Redeemer
   b. Helios
   c. Motherland Monument
   d. Colossus of Rhodes

3. Rio de Janeiro is a city in the nation of
   a. Rhodes.
   b. Greece.
   c. Brazil.
   d. Russia

4. What was the purpose of the Colossus of Rhodes?
   a. to prevent earthquakes
   b. to honor those who fought the Battle of Stalingrad
   c. to use up extra bronze
   d. to scare off would-be attackers

/4

Name _____

Warm-Up 22   Black Tuesday and the Great Depression

October 29, 1929, was Black Tuesday. On that date, the stock market crashed. During that day's trading, $10 billion in stock value was lost. Some stocks had sold for $40 per share two days before. On that day, they sold for pennies. People who had invested in the stock market went from being rich to being broke. This started the Great Depression.

In the months and years that followed, things got worse. Businesses had borrowed money from banks. They could not pay it back. Then the banks could not pay back the people who had deposited money in them. Nine thousand banks failed. They closed their doors. Most did not give back the money that people had deposited. People lost their life savings.

For the first three years after Black Tuesday, the nation lost an average of 100,000 jobs *each week*. Because so many people were out of work or afraid of losing their jobs, they did not buy things. As the demand for goods fell, businesses laid off more workers. It was a bad cycle. Laid-off workers did not buy things. So, more workers were laid off.

People could not make their home or car payments. They lost everything. Many were homeless. They used cardboard and scrap wood to make shacks. At last the government stepped in and helped. Laws were passed to prevent another Great Depression.

Check Your Understanding

1. During the years of the Great Depression, how many banks failed?
   a. The article does not say.
   c. 9,000
   b. 5,000
   d. 100,000

2. Which event occurred third?
   a. The stocks in the stock market had a high value.
   b. Businesses could not pay back loans to the banks.
   c. The banks could not pay back the depositors.
   d. The stocks in the stock market lost a lot of value.

3. What caused people to lose their life savings?
   a. They lost their homes and cars.
   b. They lost their jobs.
   c. They lived in cardboards shacks.
   d. The banks did not return the money the people had deposited with them.

4. During the Great Depression, the people who lost their jobs were
   a. able to make home and car payments.
   c. less apt to buy things.
   b. likely to get sick.
   d. investing in the stock market.

/4

Name _____

Curing Scurvy

During history, there have been times when knowledge did not get passed on. Advances were delayed for hundreds of years. For example, the cure for scurvy was discovered but not shared.

Scurvy began with aches in the joints. Often the victim's teeth fell out. Sufferers had purple blotches on their skin. They lost their minds. Then they died. No one knew that a lack of vitamin C caused scurvy.

Sailors often fell victim to the disease. In 1536, Jacques Cartier, a French explorer, and his whole crew had scurvy. They spent the winter on the shore of the St. Lawrence River. More than two dozen men had died. All the rest were dying. Then, a Native American named Domagaya found them. He used tree bark to brew tea. The tree bark had vitamin C. Every man who drank the tea got better.

Cartier and his men did not bring the tree bark back to Europe, nor did they tell anyone about the cure! Another 200 years passed. Many more people died. Then, scientists found that eating fruits and vegetables cured scurvy. In 1795 the British navy made a rule. They said that all its sailors must eat limes. This ended scurvy in the British navy.

Check Your Understanding

1. Scurvy is caused by
   a. drinking too much tea.
   b. not having enough vitamin C.
   c. a lack of clean drinking water.
   d. being surrounded by saltwater for months at a time.

2. How might Domagaya have known how to help Cartier and his crew?
   a. He recognized their symptoms.
   b. He gave them tea made from tree bark that could cure any sickness.
   c. He tested their blood.
   d. The crew told Domagaya that they needed vitamin C.

3. If someone gets scurvy, which of the following foods would be best to eat?
   a. bread
   b. oranges
   c. milk
   d. beans

4. Why were sailors so often scurvy victims?
   a. They ate too much salted fish at sea.
   b. The salt in the sea air made their lungs susceptible to disease.
   c. They refused to eat limes.
   d. They did not have access to fresh fruits and vegetables at sea.

/4

Name _____

24 The Story of the National Anthem

The year was 1812. America and Great Britain were at war. Why? The British had seized thousands of American men. They forced them to join the British Navy. Great Britain was fighting France. They needed more sailors.

Francis Scott Key was an American. His friend, another American, was a prisoner on a British ship. Key went to the ship. He had letters from British soldiers who were in an American prison. The letters said that Key's friend was a doctor. They asked for his release. The men needed his care.

The British said that the doctor could leave. But first, the British ship would attack Fort McHenry in Maryland. The men could only go after the battle ended.

On September 13, 1814, the British attacked. Key and his friend watched the fight from the ship. They saw the American flag flying over the fort. The battle raged all day and night. The men strained to see through the smoke. Who was winning?

In the morning, Key saw the American flag flying over the fort. The Americans had won! He was so happy that he wrote a poem, "The Star-Spangled Banner." Later his poem was made into a song. It became the national anthem of the United States.

Check Your Understanding

1. In 1814, the Americans were fighting the
   a. Canadians.
   b. French.
   c. Spanish.
   d. British.

2. Francis Scott Key's poem is now
   a. Britain's national anthem.
   b. the United States's national anthem.
   c. France's national anthem.
   d. Spain's national anthem.

3. During the battle, Key and the doctor were
   a. on a British warship.
   b. on an American warship.
   c. in prison at Fort McHenry.
   d. hidden inside Fort McHenry.

4. What happened first?
   a. Key brought a letter to the British warship.
   b. Key's friend (the doctor) treated American prisoners.
   c. The troops at Fort McHenry won a fierce battle.
   d. The British agreed to release the doctor.

/4

Name _____

25   *The Jungle*: A Book That Shocked People

Upton Sinclair wanted to write a book about the poorest Americans. So, in 1904, he went to Chicago. He lived among poor immigrants there. Immigrants are people who have moved from a different country. In Chicago, most of the immigrants came from Eastern Europe. They moved to America because they heard there were good jobs. But when they arrived, they found too many people looking for too few jobs. Because there were so many people wanting work, wages were low. Conditions were not safe. Workers were not treated well. If a man got hurt at work, he was fired. If a woman got pregnant, she was fired.

The factories in which meat was prepared were filthy. Sickly cattle were killed for food. Grinding machines were never cleaned. In the summer, flies crawled on the meat and the workers. Workers had to move fast. Some cut themselves badly with sharp knives.

Upton decided to **reveal** the truth. He wrote a book. In *The Jungle*, a family comes to Chicago to make a new life. But no matter how hard they work, they cannot get ahead. They suffer. When people read *The Jungle*, they were shocked. They protested. They did not want to buy meat. As a result, the government started to inspect factories. Laws were passed to make workplaces more safe and clean.

Check Your Understanding

1. Who is an immigrant?
   a. a person who works in a meat factory
   b. a person who is poor
   c. a person who comes from one nation to live in another nation
   d. a person who writes about jobs in a meat factory

2. A synonym for **reveal** is
   a. uncover.   b. hide.   c. notice.   d. change.

3. Why were workers treated poorly in 1904?
   a. The workers did not know how to do their jobs.
   b. The workers were lazy.
   c. There were not enough workers for all the jobs.
   d. There were too many workers for all the jobs.

4. After people read Upton Sinclair's book, they
   a. wanted laws to protect pregnant workers.
   b. demanded that the government inspect meat factories.
   c. quit their jobs.
   d. moved to different countries.

/4

Name _____

26   The Brownie Camera and the Photo Revolution

George Eastman did not invent the camera. But the first cameras were not practical. They were as big as microwave ovens. They weighed a lot. No one could hold one and take a photo. A camera had to be set up on a tripod. It was a stand with three legs. Glass plates and wet chemicals were used to develop the pictures.

George made a machine. It put chemicals onto dry plates. It made taking photos less messy. In 1881, he started a business. He named it Kodak. But it was still too hard to take photos. Then, in 1885, George invented film on a roll. This made taking pictures easy. People liked film. But few had cameras.

George knew everyone wanted to take pictures. He wanted the camera to be as common as a pencil. In 1900, he made the Brownie camera. It was small and light. A child could hold it. It did not cost much. Most people could buy one. George's company could hardly keep up with the demand for Brownie cameras. Soon everyone was snapping photos.

Cameras have come a long way since then. Now even cell phones take photos. It's hard to imagine a world without photos.

Check Your Understanding

1. George Eastman invented the first
   a. film.
   b. camera.
   c. affordable camera.
   d. photograph.

2. Which of these events occurred second in George's life?
   a. George invented film on a roll.
   b. George started his own company.
   c. George invented the Brownie camera.
   d. George made a machine that used dry plates for photography.

3. Because the Brownie camera didn't cost very much,
   a. a lot of people began to take photographs.
   b. George named his company Kodak.
   c. Kodak went out of business.
   d. it had to be set up on three legs.

4. If he were alive today, George Eastman might be surprised that
   a. photographs are printed on photographic paper.
   b. people still enjoy taking photographs.
   c. most people own a camera.
   d. cell phones can take photographs.

/4

Warm-Up

27

Name _____

Lyuba, the Baby Woolly Mammoth

Before the last ice age ended about 11,000 years ago, woolly mammoths roamed North America and Europe. They looked a lot like elephants. Yet they had thick, shaggy fur. We know about them from fossils and mummified remains. They lived in cold places. If one's body froze, it turned into a mummy.

In 2007, the best mammoth mummy was found. It is Lyuba. She was just one month old when she died 40,000 years ago. She fell into a river in Russia. She got stuck in the muddy bottom and drowned. Her body sank deep into the mud. This sealed off oxygen. It stopped her from rotting. Microbes formed lactic acid in her tissues. It was like they pickled her body.

Over time, the river's course changed. The riverbed where she lay turned into permafrost soil. Lyuba froze, too. In 2006, the river flooded. Erosion freed her body. She floated downstream. When the river level dropped, she was left on the bank. The next spring a reindeer herder found her lying there.

Lyuba still has her skin, hair, and some organs! Scientists are thrilled. They looked in her stomach. They found her mother's waste. Lyuba had eaten it. This would help good bacteria to grow in her gut. Elephant babies do the same thing.

Check Your Understanding

1. The name of the river where Lyuba was found is
   a. Russia.
   b. Lyuba.
   c. Mammoth.
   d. not given in the passage.

2. Which event occurred third?
   a. Lyuba became a frozen mummy.
   b. Lyuba floated down the river.
   c. The river flooded.
   d. Lyuba was left on the riverbank.

3. Why were scientists thrilled by Lyuba?
   a. She was the first mammoth mummy ever found.
   b. They didn't know about mammoths before she was discovered.
   c. Her body was in very good shape.
   d. She was the youngest mammoth mummy ever found.

4. What did Lyuba do that modern elephant babies do?
   a. ate some of her mother's waste
   b. lived in Europe and North America
   c. fell into a river
   d. shed her shaggy fur

/4

Name _____

28   Dinosaur Discoveries

Did you know that a 13-year-old girl found the first dinosaur bones? In 1810, Mary Anning discovered a huge head. It was stuck in a sea cliff. It was near her home in England. She and her younger brother, Joe, liked fossils. Fossils are ancient animals and plants that turned into rocks over time. The pair searched the cliffs. They dug out small fossils. They cleaned them. Collectors bought them. One day, Mary and Joe dug out the large head. They had never seen anything like it. Yet they could not find its body.

Then, a huge storm hit in 1812. Wind and waves knocked rocks from the cliffs. The rest of the skeleton was exposed. It was 20 feet long. It took Mary and Joe two weeks to dig it out. Years later, scientists named it *Ichthyosaur*. It had swum in the sea millions of years ago.

No more dinosaur bones were found until 1822. That's when Mary Woodhouse Mantell found some fossilized teeth. They were stuck in a rock. She showed them to her husband. He published an article about them. This began the science of paleontology.

In 2009, five feathered dinosaur fossils were dug up in China. The bones are about 151 million years old. They're much older than any other dinosaur fossils with feathers.

Check Your Understanding

1. How many years passed between the finding of the Ichthyosaur body and the next set of dinosaur fossils?
   a. 6 years
   b. 8 years
   c. 10 years
   d. 12 years

2. From this passage, you can conclude that
   a. only females ever find dinosaur bones.
   b. people have found fossils of all the different dinosaurs that ever lived.
   c. Mary Woodhouse Mantell started the science of paleontology.
   d. people are still making new discoveries about dinosaurs.

3. A paleontologist would be most excited about the discovery of
   a. fossils of 6-million-year-old plants.
   b. new findings about sea storms.
   c. well-preserved Brontosaurus bones.
   d. prehistoric pottery.

4. You can tell that floods and waves crashing on a shore both cause
   a. water levels to permanently change.
   b. removal of soil and rock.
   c. volcanoes to erupt.
   d. earthquake fault lines.

/4

Warm-Up
29

Name _____

Animal Extinctions

When an animal is extinct, the whole species has died out. Dodo birds are extinct. There will never be another one. These birds lived on just one island. They did not fly. Sailors caught and ate the birds. They had pigs on their ships. The pigs got loose. They ate the birds' eggs. By 1680, no dodo birds were left.

Passenger pigeons were once the most numerous birds in North America. At the start of the 1800s, there were about 4 billion. Yet the last one died in 1914. Why? People hunted them for food and fun. In just one day in 1896, about 250,000 were shot.

The thylacine was a small, striped wolf. It went extinct in 1930s. It had been Australia's top predator. Then sailors brought the dingo to Australia. The dingoes ate the wolf's prey. A few wolves survived on the island of Tasmania. Dingoes never lived there. But there were so few wolves left that a disease killed the rest.

Elephants were almost hunted to extinction. The British needed ivory to make balls for pool tables. Each year, 12,000 elephants were killed for their tusks. One elephant's tusks could make four to six pool balls. Then, in the late 1800s, people began to make pool balls out of hard plastic. That saved the elephants from dying out.

Check Your Understanding

1. The thylacine was a type of
   a. bird.
   b. elephant.
   c. dingo.
   d. wolf.

2. Which event did *not* occur?
   a. Dodos became extinct.
   b. Thylacines became extinct.
   c. Passenger pigeons became extinct.
   d. Dingoes became extinct.

3. How were elephants saved from extinction?
   a. Dingoes were removed from their territory.
   b. The British figured out how to make plastic pool balls.
   c. Breeding programs in zoos kept the population stable.
   d. A law made it illegal to shoot elephants.

4. How did people cause the extinction of dodos and thylacines?
   a. They brought new species into these animals' environment.
   b. They deliberately killed the animals for food.
   c. They captured all the animals to sell to zoos.
   d. They hunted the animals for fun.

/4

Warm-Up

30

Name _____

Amazing Journeys on Foot

Estevanico was African. He was sold into slavery. He worked on a Spanish ship. In 1528, the captain left him and 250 crew on the Florida shore. As they walked across Florida, Native Americans attacked them.

The men knew that there were Spanish settlements in what is now Mexico. They hoped to find one. So the group built rafts. They crossed the Gulf of Mexico. They landed in what is now Galveston, Texas. During the next eight years, they walked across the whole state of Texas! They did not find any settlers. They turned south. At last the men reached Mexico City. Just Estevanico and three others had survived the long walk.

In 1755, Mary Draper Ingles walked 800 miles. Native Americans had kidnapped her. Her husband had searched for her. Then he lost her trail. Months passed. At last, Mary escaped from the tribe. She followed a river from Ohio to Virginia. She walked all the way home. It took her 42 days. It was December and cold when she collapsed in a neighbor's field. She was close to death. Her husband nursed her back to health.

Check Your Understanding

1. What did Estevanico and the rest of the crew want to find?
   a. their captain
   b. Native Americans
   c. the Gulf of Mexico
   d. a Spanish settlement

2. Estevanico and the crew were some of the first explorers of
   a. Ohio.
   b. Africa.
   c. Texas.
   d. Virginia.

3. How long did Mary Draper Ingles walk in order to reach home?
   a. 42 days
   b. 42 weeks
   c. 42 minutes
   d. 42 hours

4. What did Mary Draper Ingles use to guide her towards home?
   a. a river
   b. a map
   c. a tour guide
   d. footprints

/4

Did You Know?

Warm-Up 1

Name _____

All About Antelopes

Did you know that there are antelopes the same size as toy poodles? The smallest antelope is a dik-dik, and it weighs up to 15 pounds. The babies drink their mother's milk for four months. Then they start to eat solid foods. They will bark when scared! They live alone in forests, eating high-protein foods, such as nuts, seeds, mice, and birds. Protein helps their brains to work. Little antelopes are smarter than big ones. They have to be to find enough food.

Elands are the largest antelopes and grow to be about the size of oxen. They live in open fields in big herds and spend their time eating grass. They are not very smart because they don't need to look for food.

Most antelopes live in Africa, and a few make their homes in Asia. Both males and females have horns, but their horns are not forked like a deer's. They have no top front teeth, so they grab grass with their back teeth. Their stomachs have four parts. Antelopes chew their food twice. They don't chew it much the first time. It comes back to their mouths for more chewing before moving from one part of the stomach to the other.

Check Your Understanding

1. Antelopes chew their food
   a. once.
   b. twice.
   c. three times.
   d. four times.

2. Adult elands are about the same size as
   a. toy poodles.
   b. deer.
   c. oxen.
   d. ponies.

3. All adult antelopes
   a. have top front teeth.
   b. have high intelligence.
   c. have horns.
   d. are about the size of a toy poodle.

4. Picture a group of antelopes grazing in Africa. What animal is sneaking up on them?
   a. a poodle
   b. a polar bear
   c. a wolf
   d. a lion

/4

Warm-Up
2

Name _____

Was James Dean's Spyder Jinxed?

James Dean was a popular movie star. He starred in three films. Then, in 1955, he died in a car crash when he was just 25 years old.

James liked fast cars. He bought a Porsche 550 Spyder sports car. He was driving it to a race, but on the way, another car crossed into his lane. The cars hit head on. James had not been speeding or doing anything wrong. It was just a terrible accident.

James' story was over. His car's story was not. The Spyder was towed to a garage. The engine fell out and landed on a mechanic, breaking both his legs. A doctor bought the engine. He put it in his car and died in a crash. Another racing car had the driveshaft from James' car put in it. That driver died, too. Two of the Spyder's tires were sold. As the driver went down the road, both tires blew out at the same time. That driver survived the crash.

The California Highway Patrol bought the shell (body) of James' Spyder for part of a "drive safely" display. It was stored in a garage that caught fire. Only the Spyder survived the flames. It went on display again. It fell off the display stand and broke a man's hip! In 1959, the body broke into 11 pieces. No one knows why. These pieces were put into boxes that **vanished**. They have never been found.

Check Your Understanding

1. James Dean died because
   a. he drove too fast and hit another car head on.
   b. a car crossed into his lane and hit him.
   c. two tires blew out on his Porsche at the same time.
   d. the engine fell out of his Porsche and landed on him.

2. A synonym for **vanished** is
   a. stolen.
   b. misplaced.
   c. wrecked.
   d. disappeared.

3. Which event occurred last?
   a. The Spyder's shell fell on a man and broke his hip.
   b. The Spyder's engine injured a mechanic's legs.
   c. Two drivers died after their cars had parts installed from the Spyder.
   d. California Highway Patrol put the Spyder on display.

4. Why do some people think James Dean's Spyder was jinxed?
   a. The car mysteriously went into gear and drove over people.
   b. The car vanished soon after James died in it.
   c. The car never won a race.
   d. Parts from the car caused a lot of injuries and deaths.

/4

Warm-Up

3

Name _____

Fleas

When you last thought about fleas, it was probably how to get rid of them. Fleas must drink the blood of mammals or birds to survive. They drink 15 times their own weight each day! They get into your dog or cat's hair and then lay eggs in your carpet. When the eggs hatch and your dog or cat walks past, the new fleas jump onto your pet.

People spend a lot of money trying to get rid of fleas. But as bad as they are, they are also amazing insects. In fact, the flea is the best jumper of all insects. It has little springs in its legs. It can jump seven inches high. It can jump 13 inches to the side, too. Most amazing of all, it can jump 600 times each hour and keep up that

pace for three days! Why? Fleas cannot fly. They need a host animal on which to live. So they have to keep jumping to find an animal.

Wild rabbits often have fleas. Adult female fleas can sense changing hormone levels in a rabbit's blood. When the flea knows that the bunny will soon give birth, she lays eggs on the rabbit. Once the baby rabbits arrive, the newly hatched fleas hop onto them. They drink the babies' blood, mate, and lay eggs. After 12 days, a few of the fleas hop back onto the mother rabbit and stay until the next time she has a litter.

Check Your Understanding

1. Why do fleas jump?
   a. They are trying to find a mate.
   b. It's part of learning how to fly.
   c. They must jump in order to keep breathing.
   d. They are trying to find a host animal.

2. Fleas eat animals'
   a. blood.
   b. hair.
   c. dead skin cells.
   d. eggs.

3. What must fleas have in order to stay alive?
   a. sunlight
   b. cool temperatures
   c. an animal
   d. carpeting

4. You can tell that many baby rabbits
   a. are resistant to fleas.
   b. have fleas shortly after they are born.
   c. eat fleas.
   d. are allergic to fleas.

/4

Name _____

Warm-Up **4**

Worms Make Silk

Silk is a beautiful fabric. It is shiny and smooth to touch. It is warm in the winter. It is cool in the summer. The ancient Chinese first discovered how to make silk cloth. But the silk itself is made by worms!

The silkworm is an insect. When it is born, it is a caterpillar. It eats a lot of leaves. Then it spins a cocoon. A cocoon is like a tight sleeping bag around the caterpillar. It keeps the animal safe as it changes its form. When it leaves the cocoon, it is a moth.

The cocoon made by the silkworm is special. It is made of silk fibers. The silkworm's body produces the fibers. The worm rolls in circles to wrap the fibers around its body. After three or four days of hard work, the cocoon is ready.

Not every cocoon has good silk. To get the best silk, people feed silkworms chopped mulberry leaves. They also protect the worms from loud noises, cold breezes, and strong odors.

To make silk cloth, humans take a silkworm's cocoon and unravel it. Each cocoon is made of a single strand of silk. It is half a mile long! Five to eight of these strands are twisted together to make one silk thread. The thread is added to many others. They are woven together to form cloth.

Check Your Understanding

1. In its first stage of life, a silkworm is a
   a. caterpillar.
   b. cocoon.
   c. worm.
   d. moth.

2. Silk thread is made from the silkworms'
   a. dead bodies.
   b. cocoons.
   c. moth eggs.
   d. moth wings.

3. To produce excellent silk, silkworms must
   a. smell strong odors.
   b. be kept in a hot place.
   c. hear loud noises.
   d. eat mulberry leaves.

4. A silkworm's cocoon contains
   a. 1 silk thread.
   b. 3 silk threads.
   c. 5 silk threads.
   d. 7 silk threads.

/4

Warm-Up 5

Name _____

Argan Oil

Argan trees grow in Morocco, a nation in northern Africa. These trees are endangered. People have cut too many for firewood. Today, the number of trees is less than half of the number 50 years ago. Yet these trees are survivors. They can survive droughts. A drought is a long period without rain. The trees can live 200 years.

Argan trees have thorns on their wide, spreading branches. They bear fruit that goats like to eat. Each fruit's pit has two or three kernels that contain valuable oil. Argan oil is one of the rarest oils in the world because these trees only grow in a few semi-desert areas.

The Berber women of Morocco harvest the oil. But they do it in an odd way. First, goats climb the argan trees. They do not mind the thorns. They eat all the fruit and either spit out or swallow the pits. But the goats cannot digest the fruit pits.

Next, workers pick up the pits that were spit out. Those pits that were swallowed are gathered from the goat droppings. They remove the pits, break them open, and get the kernels. They roast the kernels, then grind them and press them to get the oil. It takes 70 pounds of kernels to get just one quart of oil. That's why the oil is so costly.

People around the world buy this oil. Because it has a nutty flavor, some put it on salads or on bread. Other people use it on their skin or hair.

Check Your Understanding

1. Argan trees grow only in
   a. Arganland.
   b. Berber.
   c. Morocco.
   d. West Africa.

2. How many pounds of kernels yield a quart of argan oil?
   a. 50
   b. 70
   c. 100
   d. 200

3. Each argan fruit has a pit with
   a. one kernel.
   b. two or three kernels.
   c. four kernels.
   d. five or six kernels.

4. Argan trees are in danger because people
   a. have cut down too many of them.
   b. harvest oil from their fruit pits.
   c. allow their goats to eat the tree's fruit.
   d. cause droughts the trees can't survive.

/4

Warm-Up

6   Ghost Lights Over Water

Name _____

Some people have seen ghost lights appear over water. These lights have no logical explanation. People have ideas about what causes them. Their **theories** involve ghosts.

In 1752, the Dutch ship *Palatine* set sail for America. A bad storm caused wind and water damage to the ship. It was sure to sink. The evil crew killed the captain. Next, they took the passengers' cash and jewels. Then, they took the lifeboats and left. The strong wind pushed the crippled ship toward land. It ran into Block Island off the state of Rhode Island. The people on the island helped the survivors get off. Then they took everything of value from the ship and set it on fire. They did not know that a woman hid on the ship. The ship drifted offshore and burned. The woman appeared on deck. She screamed for help but did not make it off alive. Since then many have seen a glowing light off Block Island. They call it the Palatine Light.

Another ghost light appears over Maple Lake near Chicago, Illinois. Dozens of people have seen it. The reddish light glows for about one minute. It starts over the water. It floats into the woods on shore. Long ago, this spot was dry land. A man had an accident there. He lost his head. Then a lake was dug. Now people say the glow is from his lantern as he searches the water for his head.

Check Your Understanding

1. Where do people believe they see the lantern of a headless man?
   a. on the *Palatine*
   b. off the coast of Block Island
   c. off the coast of Rhode Island
   d. over Maple Lake near Chicago

2. Why did the people set the *Palatine* on fire?
   a. They wanted to have a party with a big bonfire to celebrate the rescue.
   b. They didn't want anyone to know that the ship ran aground on Block Island.
   c. They wanted to make sure it sank once the valuables were removed.
   d. They wanted to kill the woman who was hiding onboard.

3. The word **theories** means
   a. worries.
   b. speeches.
   c. ideas.
   d. tales.

4. What is known for sure about these ghost lights?
   a. No one has a scientific explanation for them.
   b. They are caused by dead spirits.
   c. The people who've seen the lights are too scared to tell anyone about them.
   d. The ghosts of people who died suddenly haunt these bodies of water.

/4

Warm-Up 7

Name _____

Chimpanzees Can Do Math!

Did you know that chimpanzees can do simple math? Scientists found that they can add and subtract using pictures. They trained the chimps to do math problems on a computer screen.

Of course, a chimp cannot read numbers. So to ask, "What is three plus two?" the scientists showed the chimp a group of three circles on a screen. Then the three circles were put into a box where the chimp couldn't see them. Next, two more circles came on the screen. They went into another box. Last, the chimp had to pick the total. On one side of the screen were five circles in a box. The other side had seven circles in a box. The chimp touched one of these boxes. Each time

the chimp got "five," the right answer, he sipped a sweet drink. This made him want to answer the questions correctly.

Chimps still chose the right answer when the displays had different-sized circles. Compared to humans, chimps were faster in picking an answer. However, they only did 91 percent as well as the people.

So, when your little brother says that math is too hard, tell him that chimps can do it. That means he can, too! It just takes practice.

Check Your Understanding

1. Compared to people, chimps can
   a. not do addition problems.
   b. do subtraction problems with better accuracy.
   c. do addition problems faster.
   d. not do subtraction problems.

2. Why do the chimps want to add and subtract?
   a. They will receive a medal.
   b. They will get more play time.
   c. They will be put in a larger cage.
   d. They will get a drink.

3. Chimps were trained to do math using
   a. pictures on a computer screen.
   b. words on a computer screen.
   c. numbers on a computer screen.
   d. actual objects.

4. Chimpanzees are a kind of
   a. bird.
   b. human.
   c. mammal.
   d. amphibian.

/4

Name _____

Warm-Up 8 Celebrity Shoplifter

Sam was a resident of Aberdeen, Scotland, and he was known for being a shoplifter. Every day, Sam waited outside a certain store. Its door was propped open. When the coast was clear, Sam walked in and took a bag of chips. Lots of people watched him do this from outside of the store. They were not police. They were customers. Why did the store owner allow this? Because Sam's a seagull!

His life as a thief began in July 2007. He walked in the open door and took his first bag. He always stole the same brand of chips. He must have recognized the bag. There are videos on the Web showing him in action.

Sam waited until the manager was behind the cash register and the store was empty of customers. Then he walked into the store, grabbed a bag of chips with his beak, and ran outside. He ripped open the bag, and the feeding frenzy began. Many gulls swooped down to eat the chips.

Many customers came to see Sam. Bringing so many people to the store meant that sales went up. The store didn't even lose the cost of the chips. The amused customers paid for them.

Scientists who study birds say that seagulls are fast and fearless. Sam's no exception. Some people view seagulls as pests. But Sam became a celebrity.

Check Your Understanding

1. Why wasn't the store manager mad that the seagull stole chips?
   a. The seagull was his pet.
   b. He didn't like cheese chips.
   c. People paid him to watch the seagull in action.
   d. It brought more customers to the store.

2. Most likely, why did the seagull always grab the same brand of chips?
   a. The manager led him to the bag.
   b. He took several different brands and this is the one he liked best.
   c. He recognized the bag and knew that he liked what was inside.
   d. The manager put the bag in a certain spot so the seagull could reach it.

3. The shoplifter in this article was stealing from a store in
   a. North America.
   b. Australia.
   c. Asia.
   d. Europe.

4. Why did people watch the shoplifter video on the Web?
   a. They hoped to see the police finally catch the thief.
   b. They wanted to see for themselves that a seagull really stole chips.
   c. They wanted to see if they could identify the thief to earn a reward for his capture.
   d. They wanted to see the store manager grab the thief.

/4

Name _____

9   A Museum Gets a Skeleton

In 1999, a right whale was found dead. Scientists had been tracking the whale. It had gotten **entangled** in fishing lines. Rescuers had cut two of the three ropes that were biting into the animal's flesh. But they couldn't get the third rope. The whale got away from them. It died from the wounds caused by the rope.

The Paleontological Research Institution has a museum in New York. It is called the Museum of the Earth. It displays animal skeletons. When the museum heard about the dead right whale, it asked for its body. The U.S. Coast Guard had towed the whale ashore in New Jersey. Workers from the museum went to the shore. They spent two days flensing the whale. Flensing is messy. The very heavy, oily whale flesh is removed using hooks and long knives. The whale weighed 30 tons. Flensing it was no easy task.

The whale remains came to the museum on a flatbed truck. Workers at the museum had to dig a huge grave. They buried the whale and covered it with truckloads of horse manure. The manure was full of bacteria and beetles. It took the tiny creatures just one year to pick the bones clean. Then, the workers dug up the bones and carefully hung each one from the museum's ceiling. Each bone is held in place with strong, clear cord.

Check Your Understanding

1. At the Museum of the Earth, a right whale's
   a. body is kept in a large saltwater tank.
   b. body is buried on the grounds.
   c. skeleton hangs from the ceiling.
   d. skeleton is built into one wall.

2. The word **entangled** means
   a. drowned.
   b. wrapped up in.
   c. sick from.
   d. harmed by.

3. What is flensing?
   a. removing the flesh from a whale
   b. digging a deep grave for a whale
   c. putting a whale on display
   d. towing a dead whale to shore

4. How did beetles and bacteria help the museum?
   a. They made it easier to flense the whale.
   b. They saved the right whale's life.
   c. They made it possible to tow the whale.
   d. They finished cleaning the whale's bones.

/4

Warm-Up

10

Name _____

Soap Nuts

Do you help out with the laundry? If so, get ready for a big change. The days of using laundry soap are numbered. Soon, you will be using little nuts to clean your clothes.

Laundry powders and liquids use petrochemicals. That means that they use up oil. We are running out of oil. Current laundry soaps hurt the environment, too. It is hard for sewage treatment plants to get all of the chemicals out of the water. These problems explain why people are excited about soap nuts.

Soap nuts are berries that grow on trees in Asia. They are picked, the seeds removed, and the seedpods are dried in the sun. No energy is wasted on processing. You put two or three of these nuts into a little bag. You drop the bag into your washer. It cleans your load of laundry. The soap nuts can be used several times. When you toss them out, they rot. This means they go back into the soil.

Not only do soap nuts clean the dirty clothes, the suds they produce are biodegradable. This means that no harmful chemicals get left in the water. They cause no pollution! You do not need to use dryer sheets when you dry the clothes, either. Soap nuts are safe for babies and others with sensitive skin. And, because they grow on trees, soap nuts are a renewable resource.

Check Your Understanding

1. What is one problem with current laundry soaps?
   a. They do not make suds.
   b. They do not get clothes clean.
   c. They are biodegradable.
   d. They leave chemicals that are hard to remove from used wash water.

2. Soap nut trees grow in
   a. the Americas.
   b. Europe.
   c. Asia.
   d. Australia.

3. Soap nuts are a renewable resource because
   a. they come from petrochemicals.
   b. more can be grown.
   c. they produce no pollution.
   d. they are safe for people with sensitive skin.

4. Soap nuts are used to clean
   a. fabric.
   b. dishes.
   c. your hands.
   d. cars.

/4

Warm-Up

11 Oil Rigs

Name _____

Oil rigs are platforms in the sea. Beneath them is crude oil. A large drill goes down through the water, then through the rock. It keeps moving until it hits the oil. The drill is taken out, and a pipe replaces it. The oil flows up the pipe and gets collected. Tanker ships come to the oil rig and get the crude oil. They take it to a refinery. It is made into jet fuel, gas, diesel, and other products.

The Arctic and Southern Oceans have a lot of ice. Large floating ice chunks called icebergs **originate** in these seas. They float into the northern Atlantic. They float into the southern Pacific. About 90 percent of an iceberg is underwater. That makes it dangerous. Ships must get out of their way. Hitting one could easily sink a ship.

Oil rigs can't get out of the way. That's why planes search every day for floating icebergs. When an oil rig is in danger from an iceberg, one of three things happens. The iceberg may be blown up. A ship may put a rope around the iceberg and tow it away from the rig. As a last resort, the workers pull up the oil pipe. They unhook the platform's chains from posts driven into the sea floor. Then they let the oil platform float out of the iceberg's way.

Check Your Understanding

1. The main idea is that
   a. planes search northern waters in order to protect oil rigs.
   b. oil rigs must be kept safe from floating icebergs.
   c. tanker ships carry oil from oil rigs to the places where it's needed.
   d. refineries make crude oil into usable products.

2. The word **originate** means
   a. sink.   c. melt.
   b. float.   d. start.

3. A better title for this passage would be
   a. "Icebergs Destroy Oil Rigs."   c. "Drilling for Oil at Sea."
   b. "Oil Rigs and Tanker Ships."   d. "Protecting Oil Rigs."

4. If there is no way to move or destroy an iceberg, the rig workers can
   a. release the oil rig from its position.
   b. jump into the sea and hope a submarine will rescue them.
   c. allow the iceberg to hit the oil rig.
   d. blow up the oil rig.

/4

Warm-Up

12

Name _____

Surviving Sailor

In May 2002, Richard Van Pham set out from California on what was meant to be a three-hour sailing trip to Catalina Island. It was a trip of just 22 miles. Instead, a sudden storm broke the mast, radio, and motor of the *Sea Breeze*.

Van Pham was 62 years old and retired. He had no coworkers to notice his absence. He also had no family to report him missing. He lived on his sailboat in the Long Beach Harbor. No one knew that he was out in the water. So for nearly four months, his boat drifted.

But Van Pham was a smart man. He drank rainwater that he collected in a bucket. He ate a sea turtle, fish, and sea birds. He even made a small grill to cook the meat on. He never knew when he would find food. So he tried to save as much food as possible.

In September, a plane flew over Van Pham's boat. He waved frantically. The pilot saw that the boat was in trouble. Two hours later, a U.S. Navy frigate arrived at Van Pham's location. He was speechless with joy. His boat had drifted about 2,500 miles. He was found 275 miles off the coast of Costa Rica.

Check Your Understanding

1. Richard Van Pham was stuck on his boat for nearly
   a. two months.
   b. four months.
   c. three months.
   d. five months.

2. Why didn't anyone search for Richard?
   a. People knew Richard wanted to be alone.
   b. Richard told others not to come after him.
   c. People thought Richard had drowned.
   d. Nobody knew that Richard was missing at sea.

3. Which food item did Richard *not* eat while on his boat?
   a. crab
   b. fish
   c. sea turtle
   d. sea bird

4. What is the most important thing someone should do before going out to sea?
   a. Eat a very big meal.
   b. Buy a new bathing suit and sunscreen.
   c. Tell people when you are going and where you are headed.
   d. Read a book about sailing.

/4

Warm-Up

Name _____

13   Missing Fortunes Underwater

Did you know that there might be millions of dollars worth of gold waiting to be found? In the past, there were many shipwrecks. Often these ships were carrying gold or silver coins. Old written records tell how many were aboard. Water does not ruin gold or silver. People want to find the coins. They may even have an idea of where to look. But finding a wreck deep under water is hard.

During the American Revolution, the French chose to help the struggling colonists fight the British. The French sent money and troops. The French ship *Griffin* had five chests of gold coins. It wrecked in Lake Michigan. The ship went down near Poverty Island. This is off the coast of Wisconsin. In today's dollars, the coins would be worth about $400 million. Many have searched. No one has found the wreck. By now all the wood may have rotted. That would make the ship even harder to find.

In 1909, the *RMS Republic* ran into another ship about 50 miles off the New England coast. Nearly everyone was rescued. Then the *Republic* sank to the sea floor. The ship's hold was filled with gold coins. They'd be worth $5 billion today. Deep-sea divers searched for years. They found the wreck in 1981. It has been more than 30 years. Many divers have tried. Still, no one has found the lost coins.

Check Your Understanding

1. Why was the *Griffin* carrying gold coins?
   a. The French sent them to the Americans.
   b. The Americans sent them to the French.
   c. The Americans sent them to the British.
   d. The British sent them to the Americans.

2. Why are people so sure that there is treasure aboard these shipwrecks?
   a. They have heard rumors about gold coins.
   b. Divers have actually found some gold coins.
   c. Gold coins have washed ashore near where these wrecks lie.
   d. Old written records say that gold coins were aboard.

3. Which event occurred third?
   a. The *Griffin* sank.
   b. The *RMS Republic* sank.
   c. The wreck of *RMS Republic* was found.
   d. The wreck of the *Griffin* was found.

4. Where did the *RMS Republic* go down?
   a. in Lake Michigan
   b. in the Atlantic Ocean
   c. in the Pacific Ocean
   d. in Lake Superior

/4

Name _____

Warm-Up

14   The World's Longest-Burning Fire

Coal mining is a dirty, dangerous job. It is one of the most risky occupations. Twenty-nine men lost their lives in a mine blast in 2010. Long ago, it was even more dangerous. And those who risked their lives did so for low pay. In 1884, the owners of the Black Diamond Mine cut the miners' pay. The miners went on strike. They would not go into the mines. They refused to dig the coal. A few of the miners lost their tempers. They soaked wood in oil. They put the wood into several coal cars. They set the wood on fire. Then they pushed the heavy cars into the mine. The cars rolled down the track and went deep into the mine. The fire spread to the coal in the mine. After a while, the whole mine was ablaze.

The men who did this started the world's longest-burning fire. It is still burning more than 125 years later. This underground fire is called the Devil's Oven. It burns in the coal veins in New Straitsville, Ohio. In the 1930s, the fire came close the surface. That's when the U.S. government sent a work crew. The crew tried different ways to put out the fire, but nothing worked. Today the fire burns about 40 feet underground. Devil's Oven has already burned 276 million tons of coal. Experts say it will burn for another 200 years.

Check Your Understanding

1. Today, coal mining is
   a. still very dangerous.
   b. an easy way to get rich.
   c. not as safe as it used to be.
   d. risk-free.

2. Black Diamond Mine was located in
   a. Pennyslvania.
   b. Ohio.
   c. West Virginia.
   d. Kentucky.

3. Why did coal miners set the Black Diamond Mine on fire?
   a. They wanted to be famous for starting the world's longest-burning fire.
   b. They thought it was a safer way to mine coal than traditional methods.
   c. They wanted to punish the mine's owners for cutting their pay.
   d. They were tired of working a dangerous job.

4. The world's longest-burning fire
   a. is still burning today.
   b. burned for 125 years.
   c. was started by accident.
   d. started in the 1930s.

/4

Warm-Up

15   Where Do Dead Satellites Go?

Name _____

A satellite is a man-made object in space that is intended to orbit Earth or another object in space. More than 2,270 satellites orbit our planet. Some take measurements. Others take photos of Earth. Many help communications. They **transmit** signals. These signals let us watch TV.

Satellites are launched into space. Each one must be at an exact height and speed. Its orbit must match the pull of Earth's gravity. This keeps it in the right place.

There are no clouds in space. The sun always shines there. So satellites use solar cells. The solar cells take in the sun's light. They change the light into electric power. The power runs the satellite's equipment.

Solar cells can last for years. But at some point, the satellite will "die."

In 2009, two satellites ran into each other. It was the first time this had ever happened. One was working. The other was old. It no longer followed commands. There was no way to make it get out of the way. It was just one of 2,000 "dead" satellites. They no longer work. They keep circling Earth.

Some dead satellites fall toward Earth. They burn up in the atmosphere. Just before some satellites die, scientists give them a command. They boost them into a higher orbit. It is called the "satellite graveyard."

Check Your Understanding

1. Satellites are powered by
   a. commands.
   b. the wind.
   c. coal.
   d. the sun.

2. The word **transmit** means
   a. organize.
   b. send.
   c. disrupt.
   d. reduce.

3. What keeps dead satellites orbiting Earth?
   a. Earth's gravity
   b. commands from scientists
   c. solar cells
   d. nuclear energy

4. You can conclude that
   a. satellites collide in space each year.
   b. communications satellites have the lowest orbit.
   c. satellites are affected by Earth's weather.
   d. the satellite graveyard is farther from Earth than the orbits of working satellites.

/4

Warm-Up

16

Name _____

Newsflash: Prey Need Predators!

Would you believe that prey need predators to eat them? It sounds crazy, doesn't it? But if there aren't enough predators to eat the prey animals, too many of them will survive. Then the prey will starve to death.

Scientists know this is true. They watched it all play out on an island in Lake Superior. In the 1920s, a pair of moose left the Canadian shore. They swam out to Isle Royale. They were the only big animals there. They had no predators. Within ten years, there were 3,000 moose! The moose ate the plants faster than they could grow back. In 1933, the moose began to starve to death for lack of food. With fewer moose, the plants grew back.

Over time, the moose population grew again.

In 1950, a pair of wolves swam out to the island. They ate the moose. The number of wolves grew. Then there got to be too many wolves! There was not enough prey. They started to starve. After many years, the ecosystem stabilized on Isle Royale. There were 600 moose and 20 wolves. There were just enough moose and just enough wolves to keep them both from starving.

Check Your Understanding

1. In what year did the moose start to die?
   a. 1920
   b. 1930
   c. 1933
   d. 1950

2. Which event happened third?
   a. Moose swam to Isle Royale.
   b. Wolves swam to Isle Royale.
   c. The moose didn't find enough to eat.
   d. The wolves didn't have enough to eat.

3. What could happen if Isle Royale had 400 moose and 25 wolves?
   a. The number of wolves would increase.
   b. The moose would eat too many plants.
   c. The number of moose would increase.
   d. The wolves would start to starve.

4. Picture a place with so many deer that they are starving. To rebalance the ecosystem, people may
   a. try to scare the deer away.
   b. allow deer hunting.
   c. put out food for the starving deer.
   d. pass laws to protect deer from hunters.

/4

Warm-Up 17 — Sinkholes

Name _____

Have you ever seen a sinkhole? It is a **depression** in the ground. It often forms when a cave's roof falls in. Another cause is when people pump out groundwater faster than rain and melting snow can replace it. A sinkhole may form slowly. It may form suddenly.

When one forms suddenly, it can be a danger. In 1981 this happened in Winter Park, Florida. Mae Rose Owens was in her backyard with her dog. To her shock, a huge tree nearby suddenly vanished! And it didn't fall over as if it had been cut it down. Mae saw that more trees were disappearing. She took her dog and fled. It's a good thing she did. The sinkhole kept growing for 24 hours. In the end, it swallowed her house, five cars, and part of a car repair shop. A pickup truck, an in-ground swimming pool, and numerous trees and bushes were gone, too. In 2007, a sinkhole swallowed 12 houses in a city in Guatemala. It is a nation in Central America.

There are sinkholes all over the world. In the U.S., they are most common in Southern states. In Alabama, more than 4,000 sinkholes have formed in the past 100 years. Scientists know places where they are apt to form. But they cannot tell when one will form.

Check Your Understanding

1. In this passage, the word **depression** means
a. a cave.
b. feeling sad.
c. a well.
d. a hole.

2. Which event occurred last?
a. A sinkhole began to form in Winter Park.
b. A sinkhole in Guatemala swallowed 12 homes.
c. A sinkhole in Florida kept growing for 24 hours.
d. Mae Rose Owens took her dog and left.

3. A sinkhole may form as the result of
a. a major flood.
b. an explosion.
c. removing groundwater.
d. building a dam.

4. In the United States, a sinkhole would be most likely to form in the state of
a. Georgia.
b. New York.
c. Alaska.
d. Wisconsin.

/4

Warm-Up

18   Spider Legs Are Incredible

Name _____

Spiders are not insects. They are arachnids. They have no ears and eight legs. They use their legs for more than moving around. Their legs let them hear, smell, and taste! Actually, their leg hairs do these things. The leg hairs are called *trichobotria*. They can feel the air-pressure waves made by sounds or movements. A spider's leg hairs are very sensitive. They know where a sound is coming from and if it's a possible meal (bug) or a threat (bigger spider).

Other hairs on a spider's legs are used to hear and taste. How? They sense tiny amounts of chemicals on a surface or in the air. These special hairs are at the base of the spider's legs. This means that spiders smell and taste the things they step on! In addition to taste and smell, some of these hairs, called *setae*, let the spider walk across smooth surfaces—such as a ceiling. Each spider "foot" has thousands of setae. Each seta has thousands of smaller hairs. These hairs are so tiny, they were just found recently. (Scientists saw them using a strong microscope.) These hairs give the spider's legs an electrical attraction to stick to surfaces. It is much like what happens when you rub a balloon on your hair and then stick it on a wall.

Check Your Understanding

1. Spiders belong to a group of animals called
   a. arachnids.
   b. scorpions.
   c. insects.
   d. amphibians.

2. A spider's setae allow it to
   a. hear sounds in its environment.
   b. walk on smooth surfaces.
   c. taste surfaces.
   d. reproduce.

3. A spider's trichobotria allow it to
   a. see in several directions at the same time.
   b. walk on smooth surfaces.
   c. feel tiny air-pressure changes.
   d. reproduce.

4. A phobia is a strong fear. Numerophobia is a fear of numbers. People who fear spiders suffer from
   a. agoraphobia.
   b. claustrophobia.
   c. hemophobia.
   d. arachnophobia.

/4

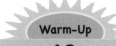

Warm-Up

19   Amazing Saving Coincidences

Name _____

In 1965, a four-year-old nearly drowned at a beach in Massachusetts. The child's name was Roger Lausier. He had wandered too far from shore. He tried to cry out, but he just swallowed water. A woman named Alice Blaise came to his rescue. She saved the drowning boy.

The Lausiers were grateful. They told Roger the story many times. Nine years later, he went to the same beach. At 13, he was big and strong. Suddenly, he heard a cry. Far out in the water, a man was struggling.

Roger grabbed his air raft and paddled rapidly to the man. The man was barely conscious when Roger reached him. He pushed the man up into the raft and pulled him to shore. The man was Alice Blaise's husband!

In 1988, Wan Weiqing saved a boy from drowning in a pond in Beicheng, China. Twenty years later, he rescued the same boy's son from the same pond!

Check Your Understanding

1. What is a coincidence?
   a. the act of rescuing a person in danger of dying
   b. the opposite of drowning
   c. an accidental event that seems as if planned
   d. being in water that is over your head

2. Why was Roger smart to use his raft to rescue the man?
   a. It was slower than just swimming out to him.
   b. The man may have been too heavy for Roger to pull to shore.
   c. A shark was attacking the man.
   d. Roger didn't know how to swim.

3. To whom were the Lausiers grateful in 1965?
   a. Alice Blaise
   b. Alice Blaise's husband
   c. Roger Lausier
   d. Wan Weiqing

4. In what year did Weiqing save the second boy from drowning?
   a. 1965
   b. 1974
   c. 1988
   d. 2008

/4

Warm-Up

20 The Janitor's Noisy Invention

Name _____

Did you know that a janitor invented the first vacuum cleaner? In 1907, Murray Spangler was a night janitor. He worked at a department store. He wished he had an easy way to clean the floor. As he worked, he thought. What kind of a machine could he make? Some ideas formed in his head. He got an old box, tape, a pillowcase, an electric fan, a broom handle, a stove pipe, and a paint roller. He added stiff goat bristles to the roller. Then he spent time making his machine. It took several weeks at home. He tried it and it worked! That night, he took his invention to the store.

Near midnight, a police officer looked in the department-store window. He saw Spangler using his invention. The officer went to the owner's house. He told him that Spangler was doing something with an odd-looking, loud contraption. The owner rushed to the store. He told Spangler that he was fired for not doing his job. Spangler told him that he was doing his job. Then he demonstrated. The man was shocked when Spangler moved his machine over dirt and gum wrappers. They vanished! Spangler sold his invention to the Hoover firm. Soon vacuum cleaners were as common as stoves.

Check Your Understanding

1. Which item was not a part of Murray Spangler's original vacuum cleaner?
   a. a pillowcase
   b. an electric fan
   c. a stove pipe
   d. a goat brush

2. Murray Spangler invented the vacuum cleaner because he wanted to
   a. make his job easier.
   b. get rich.
   c. win a bet with the store owner.
   d. help a police officer.

3. The police officer who saw the janitor vacuuming thought that Murray Spangler was doing something
   a. boring.
   b. silly.
   c. amazing.
   d. wrong.

4. The department-store owner was shocked that Murray Spangler
   a. did not give him the patent for the invention.
   b. was refusing to do his job that night.
   c. had made an invention.
   d. had sent the police officer to his home.

/4

Name _____

When Booth Saved Lincoln's Life

Robert Todd Lincoln was Abraham Lincoln's oldest son. He was the only one of Lincoln's four sons to live to adulthood. When Robert grew up, he joined the Union Army. During his army service, Robert had an accident. It was on a train platform. He would have been crushed. But Edwin Booth saved him. Edwin was a stage actor. His brother was an actor, too. His name was John Wilkes Booth.

The rescue took place in Jersey City, New Jersey. It was in early 1865. Robert Lincoln wrote about his rescue in 1909. *Century Magazine* printed his account. Robert was in a crowd. He was pushed against the train car. Suddenly, the train started to move. Robert fell into the crack between the train and the platform! Just then, Edwin grabbed his coat collar. He pulled hard. Robert put his feet on the platform. He thanked Edwin. He knew him. He had seen him act on the stage.

In April 1865, John Wilkes Booth shot and killed President Lincoln. A few months later, Robert Lincoln told Colonel Adam Badeau about his rescue. Badeau was friends with Edwin Booth. He praised him for saving Robert's life. Edwin had not known the name of the man whom he had saved. He was glad he had helped the President's son. He had felt awful when his brother killed the president.

Check Your Understanding

1. Booth saved Lincoln from being
   a. shot.
   b. stabbed.
   c. robbed.
   d. crushed.

2. Which event occurred third?
   a. Robert spoke to Edwin Booth.
   b. Robert fell between the train and the platform.
   c. Robert was standing in a line on a train platform.
   d. The train started to move.

3. Why did Edwin Booth feel better after talking with Colonel Badeau?
   a. Edwin was glad that he had helped the Lincoln family because his brother had caused it sorrow.
   b. Edwin had been hoping for a promotion, and Colonel Badeau made sure he got it.
   c. Edwin thought that Robert Lincoln would get him a job working for Ulysses S. Grant.
   d. Edwin felt certain that he would become a national hero.

4. Edwin and John Wilkes Booth were both
   a. criminals.
   b. Union soldiers.
   c. actors.
   d. editors.

/4

Warm-Up

22 Hot Dogs

In the 1880s, Charles Feltman moved to America. He came from Frankfurt, Germany. He sold cold food from a cart in Coney Island, New York. But sales were not that good. Many people preferred to eat warm food in restaurants. One day, a friend suggested he sell warm sandwiches. The friend thought that busy people might want to buy hot food from his cart. They didn't have time to eat at restaurants.

Feltman decided to sell something new. It was a kind of sausage people had enjoyed in his hometown. He put the sausage in a bun. He put mustard on it and called it a "frankfurter sandwich." People loved his creation. His sandwiches became very popular. Food sales started going up quickly. Soon, he was able to open his own restaurant.

One day in 1916, Tad Dorgan was at a baseball game. Tad was a cartoonist. The food vendors who sold the frankfurters were shouting, "Get your red-hot dachshund sausages!" This gave Dorgan an idea for a new cartoon. Dachshunds are long, skinny dogs with short legs. Dorgan drew a cartoon of a dachshund inside a bun. But he didn't know how to spell it. So he drew the seller yelling, "Get your hot dogs!" The name stuck. Now most people know this sandwich as the "hot dog."

Check Your Understanding

1. Why was Charles Feltman having trouble selling his cold food?
   a. People preferred to eat heated food in restaurants.
   b. The cold food was not cold enough for most people.
   c. The cold food did not taste very good.
   d. People preferred hot dogs.

2. You can conclude that Feltman named his sandwich
   a. after a Coney Island restaurant.
   b. for dachshunds.
   c. in honor of his hometown.
   d. in honor of baseball.

3. Ted Dorgan wrote, "Get your hot dogs!" in his cartoon because he
   a. did not like the original name for the sandwich.
   b. did not know how to spell "dachshund."
   c. wanted to be the first person to invent a name for the treat.
   d. wanted to sell hot dogs at baseball games.

4. How did Feltman probably feel when his creation became popular?
   a. glad
   b. tired
   c. disappointed
   d. puzzled

/4

Warm-Up
23

Name _____

Poisonous Plants

Have you ever had poison ivy? If so, you know that it makes your skin itch really badly. You probably keep an eye out for it when you're in the woods. You don't want to brush against it again!

But poisonous plants aren't all bad. Do you like to eat cashews? They taste good. Yet the cashew is closely related to poison ivy. The same toxin surrounds the nut. The nuts must be harvested very carefully. Sometimes just parts of a plant are poisonous. This is true of the green parts of potatoes and tomatoes, as well as peach and cherry pits.

The deadliest plant on Earth is the rosary pea. Eating just one would kill you! So people have found another use for them. They use the pretty seeds in jewelry. The berries of deadly nightshade are toxic, too. Yet the oil from the berries can save a person who eats a deadly mushroom.

Some medicines come from poisonous plants. They are given in small doses. Digitalis comes from the leaves of foxglove. It has saved the lives of people with heart trouble. Quinine comes from a rainforest tree. It cures malaria. Mosquitoes spread this deadly disease.

Check Your Understanding

1. Which statement is true?
   a. Digitalis cures malaria.
   b. Every part of the cashew plant is poisonous.
   c. Foxglove is the deadliest plant on Earth.
   d. Some poisonous plants are used for medicine.

2. Which plant has a substance that helps people with heart problems?
   a. foxglove
   b. poison ivy
   c. deadly nightshade
   d. rosary pea

3. What happens if you have poison ivy?
   a. It is hard to breathe.
   b. You sneeze a lot.
   c. Your skin itches.
   d. You have no appetite.

4. Which one is *not* poisonous?
   a. the green part of tomato plants
   b. deadly nightshade berries
   c. peach pits
   d. quinine

/4

Name _____

Warm-Up 24   U.S. State Capitals' Names

How did U.S. state capitals get their names? Native tribes named areas. In some places, the name stuck. Honolulu, in Hawaii, means "place of shelter." Topeka, in Kansas, means "place to dig prairie herbs." Cheyenne was the name of a native tribe in Wyoming.

Four capitals honor U.S. presidents. They are Jackson, Mississippi; Lincoln, Nebraska; Jefferson City, Missouri; and Madison, Wisconsin. Some capitals honor men who did something important. Richard Montgomery died in the American Revolution. His name is the capital of Alabama. James Harris ran the first trading post in Harrisburg, Pennsylvania. Kit Carson was a guide for people exploring the West. Nevada's Carson City honors him. Joe Juneau went to Alaska to look for gold. Its capital is named after him. Bismarck, North Dakota, comes from Otto von Bismarck. He was a famous German leader. Town leaders hoped to draw German settlers to the area.

A few capital cities' names come from foreign languages. Sacramento, California, is the Spanish word for "sacrament"; and Santa Fe, New Mexico, means "holy faith." Des Moines, Iowa, is French for "river of the monks." Baton Rouge, Louisiana, is French for "red stick." It refers to a red tree. This tree marked the border between two native tribes.

Check Your Understanding

1. Which city name means "place to dig prairie herbs" in a Native-American language?
   - a. Cheyenne
   - b. Topeka
   - c. Honolulu
   - d. Wyoming

2. Juneau is the capital of the state of
   - a. Wyoming.
   - b. Nevada.
   - c. Alaska.
   - d. Alabama.

3. Which capital describes a boundary?
   - a. Jackson, Mississippi
   - b. Des Moines, Iowa
   - c. Jefferson City, Missouri
   - d. Baton Rouge, Louisiana

4. Which state capital honors a famous German?
   - a. Alabama
   - b. Wisconsin
   - c. North Dakota
   - d. Nebraska

/4

Name _____

Warm-Up 25 — **Walruses**

Walruses are large sea mammals. They live in the Arctic Ocean where the water is always cold. They use their flippers and tail to swim.

Walruses eat clams on the ocean floor. It is pitch black down there. So walruses have whiskers called *vibrissae*. They use these whiskers to feel things. When the vibrissae detect clams, the walrus fills its mouth with water and squirts it. This powerful burst of water pushes the sand away from the clams so the walrus can eat them.

Like elephants, walruses have ivory tusks. People used to hunt walruses for their tusks. Now it is illegal to hunt them.

Walruses use their tusks in several ways. When they come to the water's surface, they want to lie on floating pieces of ice. Walruses can weigh half a ton each. So they plant their tusks in the ice, just as a mountain climber uses an ice ax. They use their strong neck muscles to pull themselves from the water.

Walruses use their tusks as weapons, too. They live in big groups, but sometimes they fight. The walrus with the biggest tusks wins. They use their tusks to scare off polar bears. Polar bears always avoid adult walruses due to their tusks.

Check Your Understanding

1. What do walruses eat?
   a. each other
   b. clams
   c. polar bears
   d. vibrissae

2. What happens first?
   a. The walrus dives to the ocean floor.
   b. The walrus eats.
   c. The walrus uses its vibrissae.
   d. The walrus squirts water at a clam.

3. People used to hunt walruses for their
   a. vibrissae.
   b. blubber.
   c. ivory.
   d. fur.

4. Picture a group of walruses on the ice. A polar bear is moving closer. Which walrus does the polar bear try to grab?
   a. the closest walrus
   b. the one with the biggest tusks
   c. the one with the worst whiskers
   d. a baby without tusks

/4

Warm-Up

26

Fireworks

Name _____

Do you enjoy watching fireworks? Do you like their colorful sparks and loud noises? Fireworks start out as hollow cardboard tubes filled with gunpowder. A fuse sticks into this gunpowder. The fuse is a thick cotton string. It's been soaked in saltpeter. When a flame lights the fuse, it burns the gunpowder. This makes the rocket shoot into the air. Then the gunpowder lights a smaller packet of gunpowder. This blows up the cardboard tube. It ignites tiny firecrackers at the top of the rocket, too.

What makes the different colors? Small amounts of chemicals are added to the gunpowder. Sodium makes yellow sparks. Copper makes blue sparks. Charcoal gives the fireworks sparkling tails.

Fireworks are not just pretty. They are dangerous. If they blow up near you, you can be badly hurt. That's why some states won't let stores sell fireworks. That way, only experts can set them off.

Fireworks have other uses, too. You may have seen red flares on a road around an accident. They are a different kind of firework. They burn for a long time and do not blow up.

Check Your Understanding

1. Which chemical makes yellow fireworks?
   a. sodium
   b. charcoal
   c. copper
   d. calcium

2. A firework's fuse is soaked in
   a. charcoal.
   b. sodium.
   c. saltpeter.
   d. gasoline.

3. Why are fireworks so dangerous?
   a. They produce carbon monoxide that suffocates people.
   b. They produce poisonous gases.
   c. They can blow up and hurt people.
   d. They may spread diseases.

4. Why would road flares be red?
   a. Red flares are the prettiest ones.
   b. Red flares show up well at night.
   c. Red flares are the only color that can be made.
   d. Red flares make more noise than other colors.

/4

Warm-Up

27

Name _____

Speedy Cheetahs Are in Trouble

Do you know which land animal can run the fastest? It is the cheetah, which can go from standing still to 45 miles an hour in just 2.5 seconds! They can move fast due in part to their flexible spines.

Cheetahs live on the African savanna. They hunt during the day. Their spotted coats let them hide in the grass. Then they leap out and race after their prey, which are often giraffes and antelopes. They can do short bursts of 65 miles per hour to catch a meal.

Cheetah babies look like kittens. They are born with spotted fur that helps them to blend in and hide. Even so, just one of out of ten grows up. Nine out of ten do not live to be four months old. Lions and eagles eat them.

Like lions, tigers, and leopards, cheetahs are big cats. But unlike other big cats, they do not attack humans. In fact, Africans used to keep them as pets long ago! Humans, on the other hand, have killed a lot of cheetahs. In 1900, there were 100,000 cheetahs in Africa and India. Now there are less than 13,000 in Africa. None live in India. Cheetahs in zoos rarely breed. Most often if a zoo has a cheetah, it came from the wild.

Check Your Understanding

1. When you see a cheetah in the zoo, it probably
   a. came from Africa.
   b. was born there.
   c. was once a family pet.
   d. came from India.

2. What has happened to wild cheetahs during the past 100 years?
   a. Eagles and lions have stopped killing them.
   b. Most have been caught and taken to zoos.
   c. Their numbers have dropped.
   d. They have stopped reproducing.

3. Ancient Africans kept cheetahs
   a. to ride like horses.
   b. to guard their belongings.
   c. to herd cattle.
   d. as pets.

4. Few cheetah babies
   a. have spots.
   b. survive to reproduce.
   c. have claws.
   d. drink their mother's milk.

/4

Warm-Up

28 — Skateboarding

Name _____

No one knows who first put wheels on a board and then tried to balance on it as it rolled. We do know that in the early 1950s surfers in California made the first skateboard that started the sport. They hadn't meant to invent a new sport. They just wanted to practice balancing a board on land.

Some surfers put four roller-skate wheels on the bottom of a board. They took turns riding down the sidewalk. Their name for it? "Sidewalk surfing."

Other surfers saw their skateboard and wanted one. The surfboard companies began making skateboards, too. By the mid 1960s, kids all over the United States wanted them. In 1995, the first X Games competition was held. It was shown on TV. People got interested in the sport. Now it has spread all over the world.

A skateboarder rides a board with four wheels. The person needs good balance to control the board. Most people ride skateboards for fun. Other people use them to get around town. Pro riders can win money in contests. Each one tries to do the most exciting stunt. They do spins, flips, and grinds. It takes them years of work to get that good.

Check Your Understanding

1. The main idea is that
   a. surfers made the first skateboards.
   b. pro skateboarders win money by doing tricks in contests.
   c. skateboarding was originally called sidewalk surfing.
   d. skateboarding started with surfers and has now become popular.

2. The first X Games competition was held in
   a. 1960.   c. 1999.
   b. 1995.   d. 2002.

3. What was the first name used for skateboarding?
   a. x-surfing   c. sidewalk surfing
   b. balance boarding   d. land surfing

4. Why did early skateboards use roller-skate wheels?
   a. Surfers did not want to pay for a skateboard.
   b. Roller-skate wheels were readily available.
   c. Roller-skate wheels were flexible for turning.
   d. Roller-skate wheels feel like riding on a wave.

/4

Name _____

An Unusual Relationship

Crocodiles spend lots of time in the water. Leeches swim into a crocodile's mouth. They look like flat worms. They fasten themselves to the reptile's gums. Then the leeches suck their blood. The crocodiles cannot stop these creatures. But they do know how to get rid of them.

The reptile moves up on the shore. It opens its jaws wide. This is a signal to tiny birds called plovers. The plovers **fearlessly** hop inside the big animal's mouth. They pick at the croc's teeth and gums, eating all the leeches. Of course, the plovers don't do as good a job cleaning teeth as your dental hygienist does. They don't need to. A crocodile always has a new tooth that's ready to take the place of one that falls out. This is true throughout its long life of 50 or more years.

The plovers spend a lot of their time inside crocodiles' mouths. It's a win-win situation. The crocodile gets clean gums. The birds get food. And the plovers aren't in danger from other animals while they're inside the crocodile's jaws!

Check Your Understanding

1. Why is the plover and crocodile's relationship a win-win situation?
   a. They help each other collect food.
   b. The animals are feeding each other.
   c. They help each other find mates.
   d. Both animals benefit in some way.

2. Why don't the crocodiles eat the plovers?
   a. The plovers help the crocodiles by getting rid of the leeches.
   b. The crocodiles need the plovers to bring them food.
   c. The plovers protect the crocodiles from other predators.
   d. The plovers don't get close enough to the crocodile to be captured.

3. The word **fearlessly** means
   a. feeling terrified.   c. being forced.
   b. without being scared.   d. with difficulty.

4. A crocodile is most closely related to
   a. a frog.   c. an iguana.
   b. a bear.   d. a plover.

Name _____

Frozen Boy Survives

In December 1987, Justin Bunker was nine years old. One day, he and a friend walked across a frozen pond in Connecticut. Suddenly the ice broke. Justin fell in. He lay on the bottom, face up. His eyes were shut. He didn't move. His friend ran for help. Rescue workers raced to the pond. Still, by the time Justin was pulled out, he had been underwater for more than 20 minutes.

Everyone thought that there was no hope for Justin. Yet the paramedics found a faint pulse. They wrapped him in hot blankets. They put an oxygen mask on him. They raced Justin to the hospital. For eight hours, the child lay in a bed. He was comatose. Then, suddenly, he sat up. He had survived! But how?

Doctors believe that when Justin fell into the freezing cold water, his body instantly froze. He went into a state similar to that of a patient under **anesthesia**. Doctors use these drugs to keep a person unconscious during surgery. That way, the patient does not feel the pain while being operated on.

Check Your Understanding

1. When the paramedics found a pulse, it meant that Justin
   a. was still alive.
   b. was dead.
   c. had warmed up.
   d. needed to have an operation.

2. Why did Justin have an oxygen mask on?
   a. to warm his body
   b. to help his lungs to breathe
   c. to keep him unconscious
   d. to keep him from feeling pain during surgery

3. Doctors want a patient to be unconscious during an operation so that the patient
   a. doesn't feel any pain or fear.
   b. doesn't argue with the doctor the whole time.
   c. can see what it's like to be in freezing cold water.
   d. can go without breathing for more than 20 minutes.

4. **Anesthesia** is a kind of
   a. surgery.
   b. disease.
   c. rescue procedure.
   d. medication.

/4

Fascinating People

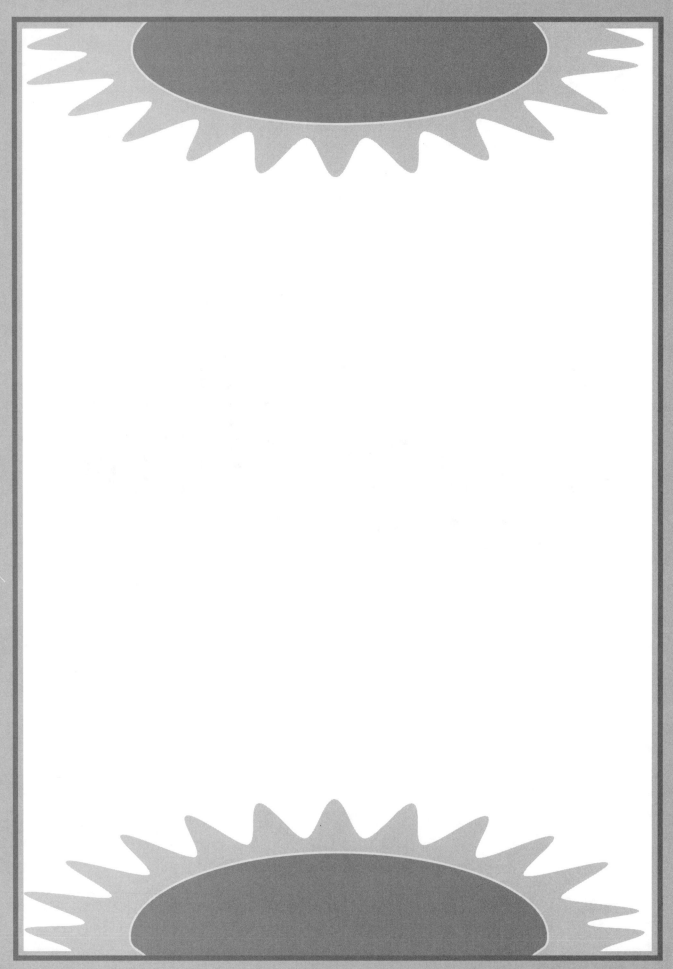

Name _____

Warm-Up 1

Susan B. Anthony, Civil Rights Leader

We live in a free country where we vote for our leaders. Yet Susan B. Anthony voted and was arrested for doing so! How can that be? She lived in a time when women could not vote.

Susan voted in 1872. At that time, only men could vote. Susan knew this was wrong. She worked hard to get women the right to vote. She traveled around and gave speeches. She told people that women should be able to vote. She said it over and over. Other women joined her, too.

After she was arrested, Susan went to court. The judge was so angry that he would not let her speak. He found her

guilty and said that she had to pay $100 for her "crime." Susan said that she would not pay, and she never did. Yet the judge did not dare to put her in jail. If he did, she would ask the U.S. Supreme Court to look at her case. If that happened, she might win. So the judge let Susan go.

One hundred years after Susan was born, all American women got the right to vote with the Nineteenth Amendment to the Constitution in 1920. People call it the Susan B. Anthony Amendment. Her dream came true, but she had died 14 years before it happened.

Check Your Understanding

1. Susan B. Anthony was arrested for the "crime" of
   a. ignoring a judge's ruling.
   b. voting in an election.
   c. giving speeches that said women had the right to vote.
   d. not paying a fine.

2. Why didn't the judge force Susan to pay the fine?
   a. The judge knew that Susan didn't have any money.
   b. The judge thought that Susan would attack him.
   c. If Susan took her case to the U.S. Supreme Court, it might say that his ruling was wrong.
   d. He thought she'd done the right thing by voting and didn't want to punish her.

3. Susan B. Anthony was born in
   a. 1820.   b. 1872.   c. 1906.   d. 1920.

4. Why is the Nineteenth Amendment called the Susan B. Anthony Amendment?
   a. The law came about due in large part to all her efforts.
   b. She asked that it be named after her.
   c. She was the senator who drafted the amendment.
   d. It was to honor her during her 100th birthday party.

/4

Warm-Up
2
Dr. Seuss, Children's Author

Do you like the Grinch? Most kids do. He is a character created by Dr. Seuss, one of the most popular children's authors of all time. Yet Seuss had a hard time getting his first children's book, *And to Think That I Saw It on Mulberry Street*, published. Twenty-seven companies turned it down. They said it was too weird. Luckily, Seuss had a friend who was an editor. His friend printed the book in 1937. It was a big hit!

Dr. Seuss did not want reading to be a chore. He wanted to write books that kids would like to read. That way children would read them over and over. So he took 220 different words from a list of 400 words that students should know by the end of first grade and used them to write *The Cat in the Hat*. It was so challenging to do that it took him a year to write it.

In his lifetime, Seuss had created more than 50 books. They have sold more than 220 million copies. And they are still selling! Which is the most popular Dr. Seuss book of all time? *Green Eggs and Ham.*

Check Your Understanding

1. What is the title of Dr. Seuss's first children's book?
   a. *And to Think That I Saw It on Mulberry Street*
   b. *The Grinch Who Stole Christmas*
   c. *Green Eggs and Ham*
   d. *The Cat in the Hat*

2. You can tell that Dr. Seuss wanted to
   a. teach children a lot of new words.
   b. write books that children would read just once.
   c. create books where the pictures told the whole story.
   d. make reading fun for children.

3. Why did *The Cat in the Hat* sell so many copies?
   a. It was hard for Seuss to write it.
   b. It told a fun story using easy words.
   c. Seuss's own children appeared in ads to get people to buy the book.
   d. Many schools required that students read the book.

4. How many different words did Dr. Seuss use in *The Cat in the Hat*?
   a. 50
   b. 100
   c. 220
   d. 400

/4

Name _____

3   Leif Ericson, Discoverer of North America

Most people think Christopher Columbus discovered America. But the Viking Leif Ericson was the first European to visit the New World. Leif was a sailor. He set sail around 1000 CE. He left his home in Norway to go to Greenland. He found Greenland covered with ice. He wondered if there might be better land further west. He set sail to find out.

Leif landed in Canada. He named it Vinland. Then he returned and told others. The next year, settlers went to build homes in the new land. Thorfinn Karlsefni and his wife, Gudrid, were two of these Vikings. While there, she gave birth to a son named Snorri. He was the first European child born in the New World.

But the Native Americans did not want the people to live there. They wrecked the Vikings' village more than once. Around 1005, the Norse people went back home.

The Norse told the story. Each generation told the next. But no one put it in writing. So, no one knew if the stories were true. Then, a Norse spindle was found in Newfoundland, Canada. A woman had used it to spin wool into yarn more than 1,000 years ago. Although many people used spindles, only the Norse had used this kind. This simple tool proves that they were in America long before Columbus set sail.

Check Your Understanding

1. What is the main idea of this passage?
   a. There's proof that the Norse people were in America almost 500 years before Columbus.
   b. A Norse spindle has been dug up in Newfoundland.
   c. Canada was originally called Vinland by Leif Ericsson.
   d. The Native Americans disliked the Norse people.

2. Who discovered Canada?
   a. Thorfinn Karlsefni
   b. Snorri Karlsefni
   c. Leif Ericson
   d. Christopher Columbus

3. Why did the Norse leave Vinland?
   a. Many of them died due to the cold weather.
   b. The Native Americans were against them.
   c. Their homes were destroyed in a wildfire.
   d. They could not figure out what crops to grow.

4. Today, Vinland is called
   a. Greenland.
   b. Norway.
   c. North America.
   d. Newfoundland.

/4

Warm-Up
4

Name _____

Barack Obama, 44th U.S. President

Barack Obama was the first African-American president of the United States. He was elected in 2008. He spent some of his childhood in Indonesia. Then he went to school in Hawaii.

Obama studied law. While he was a student, he was chosen to be the president of the *Harvard Law Review.* It was a great honor. He was the first African American to hold this position.

He worked as a lawyer. But he wanted to help the poor. So, he decided to go into politics. He thought that this would help him make the most impact. He was elected as an Illinois state senator. He worked in that role for eight years. At the same time, he taught law part-time at a college.

Next, Obama ran for a seat in the U.S. Senate. He won. He became a U.S. senator in 2005. But he did not serve his whole four-year term. Just two years later, he ran for president. He had to step down as senator to be the U.S. president.

Obama won the Nobel Peace Prize in 2009. This prize is given each year. It goes to a person who works for peace. He gave the $1.4 million prize to ten charities.

Check Your Understanding

1. Where did Obama spend some of his childhood?
a. Kenya
b. Washington, D.C.
c. Illinois
d. Indonesia

2. Of these events, which happened second?
a. Obama earned a law degree.
b. Obama was a state senator.
c. Obama was president of the *Harvard Law Review*.
d. Obama was a U.S. senator.

3. Why did Obama step down from serving as a U.S. senator?
a. He wanted to return to being president of the *Harvard Law Review*.
b. He wanted to win the Nobel Peace Prize.
c. He wanted to go back to teaching law.
d. He could not hold two political positions at the same time.

4. What did Obama do with the Nobel Peace Prize money?
a. He used it to fund a new government program.
b. He gave it to Harvard Law School.
c. He donated the money to several charities.
d. He sent it to Indonesia.

/4

Warm-Up
5

Name _____

Oral Lee Brown, Philanthropist

Oral Lee Brown was born in 1945. She went to school and worked hard. She works as a realtor, helping people to buy and sell homes. In 1987, she lent a little girl 25 cents. Brown wondered why the child was not in school. She kept thinking about her. She looked for her at a school. It was in East Oakland, California. The students there were poor. Just one out of four children there finished high school. Brown was led to a first-grade class. She did not find the girl, but she told the whole class that she would pay for them to go to college! At that time, she did not have the money to make it happen. But she knew that she could work hard and save her money.

Brown made friends with each student. She listened to them. She gave advice. If they needed it, she gave them food and clothes. Their lives were hard.

Each year, Brown struggled to save $10,000 of her own money. Then, she started the Oral Lee Brown Foundation, and people donated cash to help. Nineteen of the 23 children finished high school. Seventeen of those went to college. Most were the first in their families to get a college degree.

In 2001, Brown made the same promise to three more classes. Those students were in the first, fifth, and ninth grades. Ever since then, her foundation has adopted a new class every four years.

Check Your Understanding

1. In her job as a realtor, Oral Lee Brown helps people to
   a. learn how to drive.
   b. buy or sell homes.
   c. go to college.
   d. find good jobs.

2. Which statement is true?
   a. Brown had the money to keep her promise to the students on the day she made it.
   b. Brown found the little girl she wanted to find.
   c. People give money to the Oral Lee Brown Foundation.
   d. The Oral Lee Brown Foundation adopts a new class every year.

3. Oral Lee Brown wants students to
   a. give money to good causes.
   b. have better health care.
   c. get college degrees.
   d. start their own businesses.

4. Four of the students in the original East Oakland first-grade class
   a. did not finish high school.
   b. went to work for Oral Lee Brown.
   c. died during their high school years.
   d. finished high school but didn't go to college.

/4

6 Deborah Sampson, First U.S. Female Soldier

When Deborah Sampson was 22, she wanted to look like a boy. She secretly made boy's clothing. Then she put on the clothes and put her hair in a boy's ponytail. This was in 1782 when girls never wore pants or put their hair in ponytails.

Why did Deborah do this? She wanted to be a soldier in the Revolutionary War. She enlisted, or signed up, in the army. At that time, girls could not be soldiers. So she used the name Robert Shurtleff. She was the first U.S. female soldier.

Deborah hid the truth from everyone. She looked, talked, and acted like a boy. In one battle, she was hit in the head and shot. A musket ball lodged deep in her thigh. A doctor took care of her head wound. Then he prepared to remove the bullet. But he was called away. Moving fast, Sampson grabbed the doctor's tool. She stuck it in her wound and twisted it. She got the musket ball out by herself! She did it to keep her secret.

Deborah served in the army for 13 months. Then a fever swept through her camp, and she fell ill. A doctor learned the truth when he treated her. George Washington gave her an honorable (good) discharge.

Check Your Understanding

1. What name did Deborah Sampson use while she was in the army?
   a. Robert Shurtleff
   b. Robert Sampson
   c. Deborah Sampson
   d. George Washington

2. What did Deborah do to keep her secret?
   a. She cut her hair short.
   b. She wore glasses.
   c. She wore a fake beard.
   d. She took a musket ball out of her own leg.

3. When George Washington found out that Deborah was a woman, he
   a. let her stay in the army because she was a good soldier.
   b. gave her an honorable discharge.
   c. gave her a dishonorable discharge.
   d. had her put in jail.

4. How long did Deborah manage to keep her secret?
   a. 6 months
   b. 13 months
   c. 22 months
   d. The passage does not say.

/4

Warm-Up
7

Name _____

Jackie Robinson, Baseball Legend

In 1947, Branch Rickey was the head of the Brooklyn Dodgers baseball team. He wanted a black baseball player on the team. Back then, black and white players did not play together. They had their own separate teams. Branch wanted to change that.

Branch hired Jackie Robinson. Jackie was poor. His grandparents had been slaves. He was a great ball player. Branch told Jackie that no matter what happened, he couldn't fight. Jackie agreed.

Some people were awful to him. Even his own teammates treated him badly. They threw balls at Jackie. They called him names. They sent him nasty letters. They hit him and tried to kick him with spiked shoes! But

Jackie did not hit back. He did not call anyone bad names. If he had, people would have said that it proved that white and black players could not get along. They should not play on the same team.

Instead of fighting, Jackie played great baseball. He helped his team to win many games. He played ball for 10 years. Slowly people's ideas changed. Jackie became a hero. In 1962, he was elected to the National Baseball Hall of Fame. His uniform number was 42. In his honor, it was retired in 1997. No one on any major league team will have that number again. Plus, all major league stadiums display the number 42 in his honor.

Check Your Understanding

1. Which pro baseball team did Jackie Robinson join?
   a. Brooklyn Dodgers
   b. Cuban Giants
   c. New York Yankees
   d. Boston Red Sox

2. Why were the other players on his team mean to Jackie?
   a. They were jealous because the fans liked Jackie best.
   b. The other players did not want him on their team.
   c. They were upset because Jackie earned more money than they did.
   d. They didn't like that he got to wear the number 42.

3. How did Jackie convince his teammates that he belonged on the team?
   a. He promised to give them money if they let him play.
   b. He pleaded with them to accept him.
   c. He was a great baseball player who helped the team to win.
   d. He beat some of them up, and after that, they left him alone.

4. Why did the major league retire the uniform number 42?
   a. No one other than Jackie Robinson was willing to have that number.
   b. When anyone other than Jackie Robinson had the number, he played a terrible game.
   c. Jackie Robinson insisted that no other player ever have his number.
   d. Jackie Robinson was such a ground-breaking player that no one else should have his number.

/4

Name _____

The Fathers of Flight

Have you ever flown in a plane? If so, you can thank Orville and Wilbur Wright. They were brothers. They built the world's first airplane.

Wilbur got interested in gliders in 1896. Gliders do not have motors. They fly by riding air currents. Lots of people were trying to build a glider with an engine. The brothers decided to build a glider. The pair spent days watching hawks. They saw how the birds glided on the wind. The Wrights knew that others' planes had crashed when the wind changed its speed or direction. So Wilbur came up with a new kind of wing. It could move. If the wind changed, the glider's wings could tilt.

Next, the brothers built a wind tunnel. They used it to test their glider in different wind conditions. They made changes to it again and again until it worked well. At last they made a lightweight motor. They were ready to try their plane.

The Wright brothers went to a beach. It was in Kitty Hawk, North Carolina. On December 17, 1903, Orville flew the world's first engine-powered plane. It stayed in the air for 12 seconds. The men made three more flights that day. The longest one was 59 seconds. It was five years before people took their plane seriously.

Check Your Understanding

1. Which man was the first to fly a plane with a motor?
   a. Wilbur Wright
   b. Orville Wright
   c. the Wright brothers' father
   d. Orville Wright's son

2. Of these events, which one occurred third?
   a. The Wright brothers built their first glider.
   b. The Wright brothers made a lightweight motor.
   c. The Wright brothers watched hawks fly.
   d. The Wright brothers built a wind tunnel.

3. One of the most important things the Wright brothers did was to
   a. make a wing that could tilt if the wind changed.
   b. invent the world's first glider.
   c. build a heavy motor.
   d. create a wind tunnel.

4. When did people take the Wrights' plane seriously?
   a. in 1896
   b. in 1903
   c. in 1908
   d. in 1913

/4

Warm-Up
9

Name _____

Charles Schulz and the *Peanuts* Gang

You know Snoopy, Charlie Brown, Lucy, and the rest of the gang. But you may not know their creator. His name was Charles Schulz. He was born in 1922. In high school, he knew that he wanted to be a cartoonist. Yet the cartoons he sent to magazines and newspapers were turned down.

Schulz served in World War II. When it was over, he tried to find work as an artist. An art school hired him to correct lessons. Schulz kept mailing his cartoons to major publishers. At last, an editor asked him to come to his office. He looked at Schulz's samples. Then he agreed to publish the *Peanuts* cartoon strip in 1950.

From the start, *Peanuts* was a big hit. In fact, it is one of the most popular cartoons ever. In 1965, CBS asked Schulz to write *A Charlie Brown Christmas* and *It's the Great Pumpkin, Charlie Brown*. His animated cartoons became classics. They are still aired on TV each year.

Although Schulz died in 2000, the *Peanuts* cartoon still appears in newspapers. But no one else draws the cartoons. Schulz took just one vacation in nearly 50 years of work! He made so many *Peanuts* comic strips that they can be printed for 47 years before they start over again.

Check Your Understanding

1. When did the *Peanuts* gang first appear in newspapers?
   a. 1922
   b. 1950
   c. 1965
   d. 2000

2. Who is not a character in the *Peanuts* comic strip?
   a. Charlie Brown
   b. Lucy
   c. Snoopy
   d. Pumpkin

3. The *Peanuts* comic strip that you see in the newspaper today was created by
   a. Lucy Schulz.
   b. Charles Schulz.
   c. Charlie Brown.
   d. Charles Schulz's son.

4. How much time has passed since *It's the Great Pumpkin, Charlie Brown* was made?
   a. about 25 years
   b. about 35 years
   c. about 45 years
   d. about 65 years

/4

Warm-Up

10   Christopher Reeve, a Super Man

Name _____

In 1978, Christopher Reeve played the role of Superman, Man of Steel. With his broad smile, good looks, and bulging muscles, Reeve was the perfect Superman. He continued to act in many different roles during the 1980s and 1990s.

Then tragedy struck. Reeve loved to ride horses. In May 1995, his horse threw him. He landed on his head. He broke his neck. From that time on, he could not move from the neck down. He could not move his arms. He could not walk. He could not feed himself. He could not even breathe on his own. He could only see, blink, hear, and talk.

That's when Reeve showed his super powers. He had his house changed to meet his needs. He had a special wheelchair built. It let him move around. He worked hard at physical therapy. He trained himself to breathe without a machine for short periods. He and his wife started a new charity. It is the Christopher and Dana Reeve Foundation. It supports spinal cord research. It has raised millions of dollars.

Reeve's dream of walking again never came true. He died in 2004. He is remembered for his grace and courage in the face of great difficulty.

Check Your Understanding

1. How was Reeve injured?
   a. He took a bad fall while filming a Superman movie.
   b. He fell out of his wheelchair.
   c. A horse threw him.
   d. The article does not tell.

2. Which event happened last?
   a. Reeve started the Christopher and Dana Reeve Foundation.
   b. Reeve worked hard at physical therapy.
   c. Reeve played the role of the Man of Steel.
   d. Reeve had his house changed to meet his needs.

3. Why did people admire Christopher Reeve?
   a. He gave a lot of money to the poor.
   b. He didn't give up in the face of harsh challenges.
   c. He supported spinal cord research.
   d. He liked to ride horses.

4. After his accident, Reeve could not
   a. think.
   b. smile.
   c. hear.
   d. move his legs.

/4

Warm-Up
11

Name _____

Sacagawea, Explorer

Sacagawea was born into the Agaidika Native-American tribe. They lived in what is now Idaho. When she was 12 years old, a man named Red Arrow kidnapped her. He took her to his tribe, the Hidatsa. They lived in what is now North Dakota. One day, Red Arrow lost Sacagawea in a bet. A fur trapper named Charbonneau won her. She became his wife. He had no idea that she would one day be famous.

In 1803, President Jefferson made the Louisiana Purchase. He asked Meriwether Lewis and William Clark to explore this land west of the Mississippi River. Lewis and Clark hired Charbonneau and Sacagawea to help them. She carried her newborn son on her back. Seeing her made Native Americans accept the explorers. Both Lewis and Clark wrote in their journals that the team might not have survived without her. Why? Sacagawea knew which plants could be used for food and medicine. She asked the Shoshone tribe to give them horses and tell them how to cross the Rocky Mountains. She acted fast when a boat tipped over, too. She grabbed their supplies.

Lewis and Clark's team made it to the West Coast and back. As a result, America expanded from the East Coast to the West Coast. In Sacagawea's honor, the U.S. government put her image on a one-dollar coin.

Check Your Understanding

1. What happened in 1803?
 a. Sacagawea was born.
 b. Thomas Jefferson asked Lewis and Clark to explore the West.
 c. Sacagawea died.
 d. Red Arrow took Sacagawea from her tribe.

2. How did the U.S. government honor Sacagawea?
 a. It gave her fine horses.
 b. It gave her a boat.
 c. It put her image on a coin.
 d. It gave her a large piece of land.

3. Sacagawea was married to
 a. Red Arrow.
 b. Clark.
 c. Lewis.
 d. Charbonneau.

4. Why was Lewis and Clark's trip important?
 a. The Native Americans learned to welcome new settlers.
 b. They made maps that white settlers followed to move out west.
 c. It made Sacagawea famous.
 d. The team members learned how to speak Shoshone.

/4

Warm-Up 12

Name _____

Dr. Edward Jenner, Smallpox Pioneer

In the late 1700s, most people died if they got smallpox. But Edward Jenner noticed that the girls who milked cows (milkmaids) almost never got smallpox. One day, he asked a milkmaid about it. She said, "I've had cowpox. Most of us milkmaids have caught it from our cows. We don't get smallpox." This seemed to prove that cowpox and smallpox germs were alike. But how could this information help people with smallpox? Jenner couldn't think of a way.

A few years later Jenner became a doctor. His patients died of smallpox no matter what he did. He knew it would be best to keep people from getting smallpox. But how?

Then Jenner had an idea: cowpox, like smallpox, made a person ill. But people did not die from cowpox. What if he put cowpox germs into people's bodies? Their bodies would learn to recognize the milder germ. The body would fight it. Then smallpox germs wouldn't take hold in their bodies. After all, that's what had happened with the milkmaids.

In 1796, Jenner tried out his idea. He rubbed a milkmaid's cowpox blisters on the arm of a young boy. The boy came down with cowpox. Later, the boy was exposed to smallpox. He didn't catch it! Edward Jenner had just made the first human vaccine for a deadly disease.

Check Your Understanding

1. What is the main idea of this passage?
   a. Edward Jenner noticed that milkmaids didn't get smallpox.
   b. In 1796, a little boy proved that cowpox germs and smallpox germs were related.
   c. Edward Jenner used cowpox germs to make a vaccine for smallpox.
   d. Edward Jenner became a doctor.

2. What would be another good title for this passage?
   a. "Milkmaids Escaped a Deadly Disease"   c. "Cowpox and Smallpox Are Alike"
   b. "How Edward Jenner Stopped Smallpox" d. "Smallpox Was a Killer"

3. Which event occurred second?
   a. Edward Jenner rubbed cowpox blisters on a boy's arm.
   b. Edward Jenner proved his theory correct.
   c. Edward Jenner noticed a relationship between cowpox and smallpox.
   d. Edward Jenner became a doctor.

4. During the winter in Valley Forge, George Washington had all his troops vaccinated for smallpox. Why was this a good idea?
   a. Smallpox could have killed more of the troops than the war.
   b. Being sick at the same time would make the men bond together.
   c. It meant that the troops could infect the British soldiers they fought against.
   d. It made the soldiers have respect for Washington.

/4

Name _____

Grandma Moses, Artist

Anna Mary Moses is better known as Grandma Moses. Of course, she didn't start out life as a grandma. But she became famous around the world when she was a grandma.

Grandma Moses was born in 1860. She grew up, got married, and had 10 children. Sadly, only half of them lived to be adults. Her husband died when she was 66. To keep busy, she sewed. But it made her hands ache. Her sister Celestia told her to paint pictures instead.

So she found some old house paint and started painting. She made scenes from her memory. She liked the scenes made by the famous painters known as Currier and Ives. But her style was not similar to theirs. Her style is called folk art. Her son Hugh loved her art. He hung some of her pictures in a store in Hoosik Falls, New York. They were there for a whole year. No one paid any attention to them.

Then an art collector named Louis Caldor saw her paintings. He liked them so much that he bought them all! He knew she had talent. After he met Grandma Moses, he talked to some art **galleries**. They agreed to show her work. Her artwork was shown in books, magazines, and TV. She became famous. Grandma Moses painted until she died at the age of 101. In 2006, her painting entitled *Sugaring Off* sold for $1.2 million.

Check Your Understanding

1. The art collector who came into the store
   a. bought all of Grandma Moses's paintings.
   b. sold all of Grandma Moses's paintings.
   c. did not see Grandma Moses's paintings.
   d. did not like Grandma Moses's style of painting.

2. Art **galleries** are places where
   a. old paintings are restored (fixed).
   b. painters go to make paintings.
   c. artists are interviewed.
   d. art is shown and sold.

3. Grandma Moses died when she was
   a. 66 years old.
   b. 86 years old.
   c. 96 years old.
   d. 101 years old.

4. When Louis Caldor bought all of Moses's artwork, she was
   a. unhappy.
   b. annoyed he didn't pay more.
   c. probably surprised.
   d. certain that he'd become her agent.

/4

Warm-Up

14   Ida Lewis, Lime Rock Lighthouse Keeper

Name _____

Hosea Lewis was the keeper of the Lime Rock Lighthouse. It stood in Newport, Rhode Island. He kept the light lit. This kept ships from running aground at night. In 1858, he fell ill. His daughter, Ida, was just 15 years old. She took charge of the lighthouse. She had no idea that she would become the most famous light keeper in American history.

Ida's first rescue was four kids. Their boat flipped. Later, Ida rushed to save a soldier who fell out of a rowboat in the dark. But he had been drinking and wouldn't get into her boat! So Ida tied a rope around him and dragged him ashore. A herd of sheep and three shepherds were swept off a dock by a freak wave. Ida not only saved the men, but she saved all the sheep, as well. She saved a person who walked on thin ice and fell through, too. In all, Ida saved 18 lives during her 53 years tending the light.

President Ulysses S. Grant visited her. He thanked her for her courage. After she died in 1911, the station was renamed Ida Lewis Light. No other light keeper has ever had such an honor.

Check Your Understanding

1. Ida Lewis became the Lime Rock Light keeper when she was
   a. 13 years old.
   b. 15 years old.
   c. 18 years old.
   d. 53 years old.

2. Which event occurred third?
   a. President Grant visited Lime Rock Lighthouse.
   b. Hosea Lewis was the light keeper of Lime Rock Lighthouse.
   c. A boat with four kids in it flipped over near Lime Rock Lighthouse.
   d. Ida Lewis became the light keeper of Lime Rock Lighthouse.

3. While she was light keeper, Ida saved the lives of some sheep plus
   a. 15 people.
   b. 18 people.
   c. 53 people.
   d. 58 people.

4. Ida Lewis Light is located in
   a. Massachusetts.
   b. Maine.
   c. New Jersey.
   d. Rhode Island.

/4

Name _____

15   Crime-Fighting Granny

Did you know that the first crime-scene investigator, or CSI, was a grandma? Her name was Frances Glessner Lee. Lee hated that some murders went unsolved. She thought that there was a way to solve them. So she went to college at age 52. She became a crime expert.

Police departments around the nation asked her to train their officers. So, during the 1930s and 1940s, she made tiny crime scenes. She called them Nutshell dioramas. She used them to teach officers to find crime-scene clues.

It took Lee many months to make each diorama. She made about three each year. She hired a carpenter. He made the rooms or buildings. He made pieces of furniture, too. Lee made each doll and many of the things in the room herself. Each diorama held clues that pointed to what had occurred. Some were based on real crime scenes. Most were a blend of real crime scenes.

During a class, Lee would put a Nutshell into a room. The officers went into the room. Each one took notes about what he saw in it. Then the whole class discussed it with each other and Lee. Their goal was to find clues that might be related to the crime. Her 18 Nutshell dioramas are still used in crime-scene evaluation classes today.

Check Your Understanding

1. How many dioramas did Lee make in a year?
   - a. 1
   - b. 3
   - c. 8
   - d. 18

2. How old was Lee when she went to college?
   - a. 18
   - b. 42
   - c. 52
   - d. 62

3. Each of Lee's Nutshell dioramas was
   - a. time-consuming to make.
   - b. based on a single, real crime scene.
   - c. based on a Sherlock Holmes' story.
   - d. eventually destroyed in a fire.

4. You can conclude that Lee was not interested in
   - a. learning about crimes.
   - b. committing crimes.
   - c. creating crime-scene dioramas.
   - d. teaching detectives to identify clues.

/4

Name _____

Louis Armstrong, Jazz Legend

African Americans started a new kind of music in the 1920s. It was jazz. Louis Armstrong was one of the greatest jazz musicians. Yet he was born in a wooden shed. It had no electric power or plumbing. That's where his family lived in New Orleans in 1901. Louis went to school through fifth grade. Then he had to quit so that he could get a job. His family needed the money.

Then at age 13, Louis went to a school for African-American boys. It had a marching band. There, Louis learned to play the trumpet. He knew he had found his calling. When he left the school, he went to bars each night. Back then, each bar had a band. Louis wanted a chance to play with one.

In 1922, Joe Oliver, a jazz trumpeter, let Louis join his band. Louis was thrilled. He soon married the band's piano player. With her help, Louis struck out on his own. He started three new bands. Louis sang, too. He was a great scat singer. This means he sang syllables instead of whole words.

During his career, Louis played to large crowds in the United States. He had many fans around the world. His work had a strong influence on rock and roll. He died in 1971. The next year, he received a Grammy Lifetime Achievement Award.

Check Your Understanding

1. In order to earn money, Louis left school the first time after
   a. grade 3.
   b. grade 4.
   c. grade 5.
   d. grade 6.

2. How did Louis learn to play the trumpet?
   a. in a concert band
   b. in a marching band
   c. through private lessons
   d. He taught himself.

3. What major award did Louis receive after his death?
   a. a Grammy
   b. an Oscar
   c. an Olympic medal
   d. a Tony

4. Why do you think Joe Oliver let Louis join his band?
   a. He felt sorry for Louis.
   b. He thought Louis was handsome.
   c. He recognized Louis's musical talent.
   d. He liked the brand name of Louis's trumpet.

/4

Warm-Up

17

Name _____

Abraham Lincoln, 16th U.S. President

Abraham Lincoln was born in 1809 in Kentucky. His family was poor. They lived in a log cabin with a dirt floor and just one room. Abe couldn't go to school. He had to work on their farm. So he borrowed books and read them by the firelight. When he returned the books, he borrowed some more. He never stopped reading.

When he grew up, Abe became the 16th U.S. president. As the nation's leader, he did two important things. He kept the nation united, and he set the slaves free.

The states in the South wanted to own slaves. The states in the North wanted to stop them. So the South tried to form its own nation. This caused the Civil War. Abe read the Emancipation Proclamation on January 1, 1863. He stated that one person could not own another. Setting the slaves free let blacks join the Union forces. They helped to win the war. The nation stayed together.

Despite this, Abe was the first U.S. president to be murdered. Just days after the Civil War ended, he went to see a play. About 10 P.M. on April 14, 1865, a shot rang out. John Wilkes Booth shot the president in the back of his head. Booth had sided with the South in the War.

Check Your Understanding

1. Abe Lincoln died in
   a. 1809.
   b. 1863.
   c. 1865.
   d. 1867.

2. The Civil War was a fight between
   a. states in the South and states in the North.
   b. Great Britain and the United States.
   c. slaves and their owners.
   d. slaves and the United States.

3. What happened third?
   a. Abe set the slaves free with the Emancipation Proclamation.
   b. The North won the Civil War.
   c. Abe was elected as U.S. president.
   d. John Wilkes Booth shot Abe.

4. Why did John Wilkes Booth shoot Abe Lincoln?
   a. He blamed the president for the fact that the South had had slaves.
   b. He didn't like the fact that the North had won the war.
   c. He wanted to be the U.S. president and thought killing Abe would let him take over.
   d. He did not want to be a Civil War soldier.

/4

Warm-Up

18   Walt Disney Changes Entertainment

Name _____

When Walt Disney was born in 1901, no one knew that one day, his name would be a household word. He would forever change entertainment, first in the United States, and later in the world.

As a child, Walt was poor. He lived in a big family on a farm in Missouri. Even when he was small, he liked to draw.

Walt quit school after ninth grade. He wanted to be a soldier in World War I. But he was too young. So he drove a Red Cross ambulance in France. After the war ended, Walt and a friend formed an art company. They made a few silent animated (moving) cartoons.

In 1923, Walt and his brother Roy started Walt Disney Productions. Soon Walt made a new character. He called him Mortimer Mouse. His wife, Lillian, hated the name. The couple did not argue often. But they fought for a long time about that name. At last Walt gave in. In 1928 Mickey Mouse starred in *Steamboat Willie*. It was the world's first cartoon with **synchronized** sound. This means that the sound matched the actions in the film.

From the start, people loved Mickey. Soon Walt made friends for him. He came up with Donald Duck, Pluto, Minnie Mouse, and Goofy. Walt made the world's first feature-length animated movie. It was *Snow White and the Seven Dwarfs*. Walt earned more than 30 Academy Awards for his work.

Check Your Understanding

1. What was the name of Walt's first feature-length animated film?
   a. *Steamboat Willie*   c. *Donald Duck*
   b. *Mickey Mouse*   d. *Snow White and the Seven Dwarfs*

2. The word **synchronized** means
   a. at the same time.   c. loud.
   b. animated.   d. handmade.

3. Who was the star of the cartoon *Steamboat Willie*?
   a. Goofy   c. Mickey
   b. Pluto   d. Willie

4. Why did Walt finally agree to change Mortimer's name to Mickey?
   a. The name Mickey has more syllables than Mortimer.
   b. The name Mickey has the same number of letters as the word *mouse*.
   c. His wife did not like the name Mortimer.
   d. His wife said she would leave him if he didn't change the name.

/4

Warm-Up

19

Name _____

Zhang Yin, Rich Recycler

Zhang Yin is the richest person in China. In fact, she is one of the richest people on Earth. She is worth $3.4 billion. And she made all that money herself. How? She started a company. It is Nine Dragons Paper Holdings. Her company buys scrap paper from the U.S. and Europe. The paper goes to China. There, Yin uses it to make cardboard boxes. The boxes are used to pack Chinese goods. Most of these goods are **exported**. They are sold to other nations. Yin's company is China's biggest paper maker. Her business is growing so fast, it will soon be the largest paper maker in the world. Yin calls herself "The Empress of Waste Paper."

Yin was one of eight children. She was not born rich. Nor was she given any money. She is the richest self-made woman on Earth. "Self-made" means that she earned the money herself. She is even richer than Oprah Winfrey and J. K. Rowling. Like Yin, those women started out poor. They made their own fortunes.

Yin has proven the truth in the saying, "One person's trash is another person's treasure." Her company helps the environment, too. Each piece of paper she recycles slows the cutting of forests. In 2007, her company recycled 65 million metric tons. This left 57 million metric tons of trees alive.

Check Your Understanding

1. What is the name of Zhang Yin's company?
   a. Zhang Yin Recycling
   b. The Empress of Waste Paper
   c. Nine Dragons Paper Holdings
   d. Nine Dragons Paper Recycling

2. The word **exported** means
   a. sent out of the country.
   b. kept in the country.
   c. brought into the country.
   d. recycled.

3. What do Zhang Yin, Oprah Winfrey, and J. K. Rowling have in common?
   a. These women are all writers.
   b. These women own recycling businesses.
   c. These women started life poor and then made a lot of money.
   d. These women are equally rich.

4. From where does Yin's company buy scrap paper?
   a. Europe and China
   b. Europe and the United States
   c. the United States and China
   d. the United States and India

/4

Name _____

Warm-Up 20 — Heroic Chiune Sugihara

Chiune Sugihara was a Japanese diplomat. He lived in an embassy in Lithuania. In July 1940, hundreds of Jews fled from Poland. They came to Sugihara. They asked him to write them visas to Japan. The Nazis were coming, and they wanted to kill the Jews. But the people could not leave the nation without visas. They were trapped.

Three times Sugihara asked the Japanese government for permission to write these visas. Each time he was refused. He talked to his wife, two small sons, and sister. They discussed what to do. Sugihara decided to write the visas to save the people. His family agreed. If caught, he and his family would face jail or death.

Each visa had to be handwritten. Sugihara wrote from dawn to dark. His arm hurt. His shoulder ached. Still, he kept writing. He did not let his wife or sister write one. He wanted to take full responsibility. He hoped that he would be the only one punished.

The whole Sugihara family went to jail for 18 months. When they got out, Sugihara was fired for writing the visas. He would never again work for the Japanese government.

This brave man had saved the lives of more than 6,000 Jews. His courage earned him the Righteous Among the Nations Award in 1985. Today, there is a monument in Japan that honors him.

Check Your Understanding

1. Chiune Sugihara was originally from
   a. Poland.
   b. the United States.
   c. Japan.
   d. Lithuania.

2. By writing visas for the Jews, Sugihara was disobeying
   a. the Japanese government.
   b. the Lithuanian government.
   c. international laws.
   d. the Nazis.

3. Most of the Jews for whom Sugihara wrote visas
   a. sold the visas to the Nazis.
   b. used the visas to leave Lithuania.
   c. sold the visas on the black market.
   d. used the visas to get out of jail.

4. Did Sugihara's plan for writing all the visas himself work?
   a. No, his whole family was jailed for a year and a half.
   b. No, no Jews escaped using his visas.
   c. Yes, only he had to go to jail when he was caught.
   d. Yes, he was not allowed to work for his government ever again.

/4

Warm-Up

21   **Harry Houdini, Master Magician**

Name _____

Harry Houdini was born in Hungary in 1874. His family moved to the United States when he was very young. He and his brothers set up simple magic shows on street corners to earn money. Harry had an amazing imagination. He thought up new, daring tricks.

When he grew up, Harry became the most famous magician to ever live. Many of his escapes were very daring. He could have easily died. Once he swallowed needles and thread. Then he was buried in a coffin on stage. Within two minutes, he had escaped and spit out the needles and thread. He got free of every set of handcuffs ever put on him. He escaped from being held upside down in a box full of water. He got out of a nailed-shut packing crate and a large milk can. It was full of water and padlocked shut. No ropes could hold him for more than a few minutes.

A daring escape did not kill Harry. A magic trick did not kill Harry. A fan did! In 1926, Harry had a swollen appendix. He felt ill. Still, he put on a show. He had said that his stomach was like steel. After the show, a fan punched Harry in the gut. It made his appendix burst. The world mourned the great magician.

Check Your Understanding

1. One time, Harry escaped from a buried
   a. milk can.
   b. packing crate.
   c. suitcase.
   d. coffin.

2. Where was Harry born?
   a. Hungary
   b. United States
   c. Canada
   d. Russia

3. How did Harry die?
   a. He drowned during a trick.
   b. His appendix burst.
   c. He bled to death.
   d. He suffocated during a trick.

4. Why was Harry so famous?
   a. He would dance during his magic shows.
   b. He could read people's minds.
   c. He did many amazing magic tricks.
   d. He could hold his breath longer than anyone else.

/4

Name _____

Warm-Up 22   Dat So La Lee, Basket Weaver

You are looking into the past. You see an old woman. She is sitting down. She is looking intently at something in her lap. Her fingers move fast. She weaves together strips of willow, birch, and fern. Now you see it: She is making a basket. Its design is complex. Each strip must be carefully placed to form the pattern. You hold up a magnifying glass. You peer at the basket. There are no flaws! Who was this amazing artist? Dat So La Lee.

Dat So La Lee was one of the Washoe tribe. She lived in Nevada. She is a famous Native-American artist. The designs she made on baskets are beautiful. Abe and Amy Cohn were stunned at her work. When she was about 85, they built her a small house. She lived there and made baskets. The couple helped her to sell them. Back then, her baskets sold for $1,000 each. That was a fortune in the early 1900s.

Her tribe called her the "Queen of the Washoe Basket Makers." During her life, she made more than 250 baskets. She died in 1925. Now museums display many of her baskets. One of them recently sold for more than $250,000. They are the most valuable Native-American baskets in the world.

Check Your Understanding

1. What tribe was Dat So La Lee born into?
   a. Navajo
   b. Washoe
   c. Nevada
   d. Solalee

2. During her life, about how many baskets did Dat So La Lee weave?
   a. 75
   b. 100
   c. 250
   d. 925

3. Which of these woods did she use in her weaving?
   a. willow
   b. oak
   c. maple
   d. ash

4. Why are Dat So La Lee's beautiful baskets so valuable?
   a. They are so old.
   b. There will never be any more like them made.
   c. They are the biggest baskets in the world.
   d. They are stronger than other woven baskets.

/4

Warm-Up
23

Name _____

Joe Louis, the Brown Bomber

Joe Louis was an African American. He was born in the South in 1914. He was one of eight kids. His family lived in a shack. It had no windows or electric power. In 1926, they moved to Detroit. Joe met some boys. They liked to box. He found he was good at the sport. His mother did not want him to box. She wanted him to play the violin. He hid his boxing gloves inside its case.

He took a factory job. He kept boxing on the weekends. Joe lost a fight to a former Olympic fighter. He almost quit. Then, a businessman offered to pay Joe to box. He got a coach to train him. Joe won his first 22 heavyweight fights. Then he lost a few matches. Between the years of 1937 and 1949, Joe defended his title of world heavyweight champion 25 times. He did not lose even once!

During World War II, Joe was in the Army. The "Brown Bomber" kept boxing and winning. He gave most of his prize money to the war effort. He was a U.S. hero. When the war ended, he kept **donating** much of his prize money. He gave to schools.

Joe died in 1981. But he's not been forgotten. In 2005, the International Boxing Research Organization named Joe the greatest heavyweight boxer of all time.

Check Your Understanding

1. How many times did Joe defend his heavyweight title without a single loss?
   a. 25
   b. 26
   c. 37
   d. 49

2. What did Joe's mother want her son to do?
   a. work in a factory
   b. join the Navy
   c. box
   d. play the violin

3. What does **donating** mean?
   a. keeping
   b. rejecting
   c. giving away
   d. earning

4. What did Joe do with his prize money?
   a. used it to help the war effort and schools
   b. invested in the stock market
   c. bought weapons
   d. took violin lessons

/4

Warm-Up

24

Name _____

Supermex, the Pro Golfer

Lee Trevino is Latino. He was born in Dallas, Texas, in 1939. He lived with his mother and his grandfather in a shed. It did not have windows or running water.

One day, Lee saw people playing golf. He found that he could earn money by finding lost golf balls. He sold them to the golfers. At the age of eight, he became friends with the groundskeeper of the golf course. The two of them looked for lost golf balls. The next year, Lee became a caddie. This means that he carried golfers' clubs. After work, Lee played golf with other caddies. They used an old set of clubs that had been thrown out. This was Lee's only golf training.

Lee left school at the age of 14. He got a job helping to maintain a golf course. When he was old enough, he joined the Marines. There, his amazing golf talent was noticed. In 1967, he played in his first Professional Golf Association (PGA) tour. He won the U.S. Open the next year. People called him "Supermex."

Lee was struck by lightning during the 1975 U.S. Open. He was hurt. But he came back better than ever. During his career, Lee had 89 professional golf wins, 29 PGA tour wins, and six major championships. *Golf Digest* ranked Lee as the 14th-greatest golfer ever.

Check Your Understanding

1. At what age did Lee leave school to work on a golf course?
   a. 8 years old
   b. 14 years old
   c. 17 years old
   d. 18 years old

2. Where was Lee born?
   a. Dallas
   b. Atlanta
   c. Mexico
   d. Houston

3. Lee first won the U.S. Open in
   a. 1959.
   b. 1967.
   c. 1968.
   d. 1975.

4. Why do people call Lee "Supermex"?
   a. He is a strong golfer and Mexican chef.
   b. He is very strong and was born in Mexico.
   c. He is a strong golfer with a Mexican wife.
   d. He is a strong golfer with Mexican ancestors.

/4

Name _____

The Female Moses

Harriet Tubman was born a slave around 1820. Her parents and ten siblings lived in a one-room hut with a dirt floor. By the time she was eight, she worked all day. When she was a teen, Harriet stepped between a master and a runaway slave. The master hit her in the head with a heavy iron. She decided she would be free or die trying.

In 1844, Harriet married John Tubman. She told him that she wanted to escape. He threatened to tell her master! So Harriet ran away alone. A white woman had told Harriet that she would help her. So she went there one night. There,

Harriet learned about the Underground Railroad. Each day, she hid at one of these homes. She walked at night until she reached a state where she could be free.

During the next ten years, she made 19 trips back to the slave states. She led 300 people to freedom on the Underground Railroad. Men were always trying to catch them. But she never lost anyone who started out with her. People called her "Moses" because she led her people out of slavery.

Check Your Understanding

1. What was the Underground Railroad?
   a. A railroad built under the ground.
   b. Places like woods and streams where it was safe to hide.
   c. People who hid slaves in their homes or barns.
   d. The first railroad built by slaves in the early 1800s.

2. What happened last?
   a. Harriet ran away.
   b. Harriet got married.
   c. Harriet found out about the Underground Railroad.
   d. Harriet led other slaves to freedom.

3. How many times did Harriet "ride" the Underground Railroad?
   a. 19　　　　　　　　　　　　c. 10
   b. 20　　　　　　　　　　　　d. 300

4. Picture Harriet with a group she's guiding. It's daytime, so they're hiding in a Southern swamp. What animal do they need to watch out for?
   a. an elephant
   b. a shark
   c. a polar bear
   d. an alligator

/4

Name _____

Warm-Up

26   Brave Irena Sendler

In September 1939, the Nazis invaded Poland. They trapped 350,000 Jews in the Warsaw Ghetto. This area was walled off and guarded. The Jews had little access to medical care.

Irena Sendler was a Christian. She joined a secret group to help the Jews. She told the Germans that she had medicine for the people in the Ghetto. The Nazis let her in. They did not want diseases to spread to the rest of the city.

With the help of ten others, Irena snuck 2,500 children to safety. She smuggled babies out in cars, toolboxes, and potato sacks. Volunteers crawled with children through sewer pipes. The people who took in the children were brave. If discovered, the whole family could be killed.

For 16 months, Irena worked to save the children. Then the Nazis found out. They demanded that she tell where the children were placed. But she refused to speak. For this, she was badly hurt. They broke both of her feet. Then they broke both of her legs! She was in awful pain. Still she did not speak. They sentenced her to death, but she was snuck out of jail. She lived to be 98. Due to her injuries, she had trouble walking for the rest of her life.

Check Your Understanding

1. How many people helped Irena to smuggle children from the Warsaw Ghetto?
   a. 10
   b. 25
   c. 39
   d. 100

2. About how many Jews were trapped in the Warsaw Ghetto?
   a. 16,000
   b. 98,000
   c. 250,000
   d. 350,000

3. In what year did the Nazis invade Poland?
   a. 1916
   b. 1925
   c. 1939
   d. 1998

4. Why did the Nazis break Irena's legs and feet?
   a. They wanted to punish her for lying to them.
   b. They expected her to tell where the children were living.
   c. They wanted to correct a medical problem she had.
   d. They were doing experiments with bones.

 /4

Warm-Up 27

Name _____

Golda Meir, Israel's Heroine

Golda Meir was a Jew. She was born in Russia. At that time, the Russian army would attack Jewish towns with no warning. They would beat people to death and burn down houses. It was an awful time. So Golda and her family fled. They went to the United States.

Golda and her husband went to Palestine in the 1920s. It is in the Middle East. Many Jews lived there. Golda wanted to help them. Great Britain was in charge of the nation. Food was hard to get. Medical care was scarce. People lived in homes that were falling apart. But Golda did not go back to the United States. She stayed and lived in the poor conditions. She wanted to help.

Israel is the Jewish homeland. It was once a part of Palestine. In 1948, Israel became its own nation. Right away, five other nations attacked it. Israel fought back and survived. It was attacked again in 1967. During these wars, Golda was part of the Israeli government. Then she retired. But the public wouldn't let her go. They begged her to lead their country. So she became the prime minster (like a president) when she was 70 years old. She led her nation to victory during a 1973 war.

Golda died in 1978. She is one of the most admired women in history.

Check Your Understanding

1. In what year did Israel become a nation?
   a. 1920
   b. 1948
   c. 1967
   d. 1973

2. Where was Golda Meir born?
   a. Russia
   b. Palestine
   c. Great Britain
   d. United States

3. What top leadership role did Golda Meir hold in Israel?
   a. chief executive officer
   b. queen
   c. prime minister
   d. president

4. Why did Golda go to Palestine?
   a. It had better weather than Russia.
   b. She wanted to help the Jewish people there.
   c. The area is known for its religious freedom.
   d. The United States made her leave.

/4

Warm-Up
28 Franklin Chang-Díaz, Astronaut and Physicist

Name _____

Franklin Chang-Díaz was born in Costa Rica. When he was small, he dreamed of being an astronaut. He and his friends found a big cardboard box. They cut holes in it for windows. They got inside. They pretended like it was a spaceship. While he was a boy, Franklin looked at the night sky. He hoped to see the little bright moving dot that was *Sputnik*. It was the world's first satellite. The Soviet Union launched it in 1957.

Franklin finished high school. Then he went to college in the United States. He worked hard to pay his way through school. He got a degree in physics. In 1980, he joined NASA. He was a physicist. Then he trained to be an astronaut. He was the first Latino astronaut. His first flight was in 1986. He went up in the space shuttle *Columbia*. He did experiments. Before he left NASA, Franklin went on seven space-shuttle missions. (He is tied with another astronaut for the most spaceflights.)

Today, Franklin is the president of Ad Astra Rocket Company. His company designs space rockets. He wants to build a rocket that will cut the time it takes to reach Mars in half. Right now, the best rockets take eight months to reach Mars. Franklin talks with students, too. He encourages them to be scientists and astronauts.

Check Your Understanding

1. Which nation launched *Sputnik*?
   a. Soviet Union
   b. China
   c. Costa Rica
   d. United States

2. Right now, about how long do rockets take to reach Mars?
   a. 2 weeks
   b. 80 days
   c. 4 months
   d. 8 months

3. What was Franklin the first to do?
   a. see *Sputnik* in space
   b. be a Latino astronaut
   c. be a president of a company
   d. send a rocket to Mars

4. What do astronauts do as part of their jobs?
   a. build rocket engines
   b. repair rocket engines
   c. do experiments in space
   d. teach science to children

/4

Name _____

The Tale of Beatrix Potter

Beatrix Potter was born in 1866. She lived in London, England. Her family spent their vacations in rural parts of England and Scotland. There, Beatrix developed a love of wild animals. She spent hours watching bunnies, squirrels, and birds. She painted watercolor pictures of them, too.

When Beatrix was 27, she sent some illustrated stories about a rabbit to a sick boy. She wanted to cheer him up. The boy's mother had the text of the stories printed in 1900. She called the book *The Tale of Peter Rabbit.* The book was just for her son, but she showed it to many people.

Within a year, a publisher named Norman Warne saw it. He told Beatrix he wanted to print the book for the public. He asked if she had pictures. When she showed them to him, he was thrilled. He printed her book with its pictures. It was a big hit.

Beatrix fell in love with Norman. They were to be married. But he died before their wedding. It took her many years to get over his death. Beatrix also wrote *The Tale of Squirrel Nutkin, Benjamin Bunny*, and *Mr. Jeremy Fisher*. Many of her 23 books are still in print. You may have read some of them. *The Tale of Peter Rabbit* is the most popular.

Check Your Understanding

1. Where did Beatrix Potter grow up?
   a. in Scotland
   b. in Ireland
   c. in England
   d. in France

2. How old was Beatrix when she wrote *The Tale of Peter Rabbit*?
   a. 18 years old
   b. 27 years old
   c. 53 years old
   d. 66 years old

3. Who published *The Tale of Peter Rabbit* for the public?
   a. Norman Warne
   b. Jeremy Fisher
   c. Peter Nutkin
   d. Benjamin Bunner

4. Think about when Beatrix wrote her stories. What kind of adventures might her animal characters have had?
   a. using a computer
   b. driving a car
   c. flying in a plane
   d. escaping from a hunter

/4

Name _____

30   Fannie Farmer Changes Cooking

Fannie Farmer lived in Massachusetts. She wanted to go to college. But when she was just 16, she had a stroke. After that, she had to learn how to walk again. She gave up her college plans. Instead, she helped her mother to cook. Fannie found that she was a great cook.

Fannie went to Boston Cooking School. She was a strong student. She was soon made the assistant director of the school. When she was 37, she became the school's leader. She came up with the modern recipe. How? Fannie was frustrated by recipes in the late 1800s. There were no measurements included! Instead, they were written in words such as "Mix together a fistful of flour and lard (fat) the size of a hen's egg."

Fannie rewrote recipes. She used exact measurements. She told how many cups and tablespoons. In 1896, she asked a publisher to print her *Boston Cooking School Cookbook*. The publisher said it wouldn't sell. Fannie had to pay for the book to be printed. It became a bestseller almost overnight! Today, the book is still in print. Its title is *The Fannie Farmer Cookbook*. Her cookbook has been in print for more than 100 years.

Later, Fannie made special diets for people with health problems. In this way, she started the field of nutrition science. She taught at Harvard Medical School.

Check Your Understanding

1. How old was Fannie Farmer when she became the director of the Boston Cooking School?
   a. 18 years old   c. 46 years old
   b. 37 years old   d. 51 years old

2. What title did Fannie Farmer write in 1896?
   a. *The Fannie Farmer Book*   c. *The Farmer Cookbook*
   b. *Nutrition Science*   d. *Boston Cooking School Cookbook*

3. Why were recipes hard to follow before Fannie?
   a. Few recipes were written down.
   b. There were no exact measurements given.
   c. Almost no one could read.
   d. Recipes did not tell the ingredients.

4. What is the main job of a nutritionist?
   a. to make diets for people with health issues
   b. rewriting cookbooks with exact measurements
   c. to create cookbooks
   d. to teach at a cooking school

/4

Answer Key

Answer Key

Interesting Places and Events

page 9   Racing to the South Pole
1. d
2. c
3. c
4. a

page 10   Without a Trace
1. d
2. b
3. c
4. a

page 11   Mysterious Rock Monuments
1. a
2. c
3. a
4. b

page 12   Alaska, America's Final Frontier
1. a
2. b
3. d
4. c

page 13   The First Climb Up Mount Everest
1. c
2. d
3. b
4. c

page 14   The Triangle Shirtwaist Fire
1. b
2. d
3. c
4. b

page 15   Saved by the Ringtones
1. a
2. d
3. c
4. b

page 16   The Galveston Hurricane of 1900
1. b
2. d
3. b
4. c

page 17   The Bridge that Lasted Four Months
1. a
2. c
3. a
4. b

page 18   Deadly Mudflows in South America
1. d
2. c
3. a
4. c

page 19   The Mysterious Rocks of Racetrack Playa
1. a
2. b
3. d
4. c

page 20   The First Moon Landing
1. c
2. b
3. d
4. a

page 21   The Klondike Gold Rush
1. a
2. c
3. d
4. b

page 22   The Lake on the Mountain
1. a
2. d
3. c
4. c

page 23   A Perfect Emergency Landing
1. b
2. d
3. a
4. b

page 24   Colorado River Adventure
1. c
2. a
3. d
4. b

page 25   The High Desert
1. c
2. b
3. a
4. d

page 26   Finding a Missing Masterpiece
1. b
2. a
3. b
4. d

page 27   The Everglades
1. c
2. b
3. a
4. b

page 28   The First Transatlantic Flight
1. a
2. b
3. c
4. d

page 29   The City of Water
1. a
2. b
3. c
4. d

page 30   The Dead Sea
1. c
2. b
3. d
4. a

page 31   Earth's Hot Spots
1. d
2. b
3. c
4. d

page 32   The *Hindenburg* Disaster
1. c
2. d
3. c
4. b

page 33   Spooky Places in North Carolina
1. b
2. c
3. b
4. a

page 34   The World's Tallest Building
1. d
2. d
3. c
4. b

page 35   The Battle of Midway Island
1. b
2. d
3. c
4. b

page 36   Where Is Atlantis?
1. d
2. d
3. b
4. c

page 37   What's Hidden on Oak Island?
1. c
2. c
3. b
4. a

Answer Key *(cont.)*

page 38 The Great Race of Mercy
1. b
2. c
3. b
4. d

Scientifically Speaking

page 41 Your Genes
1. b
2. a
3. d
4. b

page 42 Bird Migration
1. a
2. a
3. c
4. b

page 43 Toads
1. b
2. d
3. c
4. a

page 44 The Very Unusual Parrotfish
1. d
2. a
3. c
4. b

page 45 Common Bugs in Your Backyard
1. d
2. c
3. b
4. a

page 46 Head Lice
1. c
2. b
3. a
4. d

page 47 Similarities Among Mammals
1. b
2. a
3. c
4. d

page 48 Heat
1. a
2. d
3. b
4. c

page 49 Smart Animals
1. b
2. a
3. c
4. d

page 50 Chelonians
1. a
2. d
3. c
4. b

page 51 Can You Hear That?
1. d
2. b
3. c
4. a

page 52 Salmon
1. a
2. d
3. c
4. a

page 53 Our Moon Came From Earth
1. c
2. a
3. d
4. b

page 54 Escaping From Predators
1. c
2. d
3. a
4. c

page 55 Wind Patterns
1. c
2. a
3. d
4. b

page 56 Earthworms Improve Soil
1. d
2. b
3. d
4. a

page 57 Rabbits
1. d
2. b
3. a
4. c

page 58 Don't Spread Germs!
1. a
2. d
3. b
4. c

page 59 Unusual Mother Animals
1. c
2. d
3. d
4. a

page 60 Ospreys, Expert Fishers
1. b
2. c
3. d
4. a

page 61 Meteors
1. a
2. c
3. b
4. b

page 62 Clever Animal Traps
1. a
2. d
3. c
4. b

page 63 Earthquakes
1. c
2. d
3. a
4. b

page 64 The Great Pacific Garbage Patch
1. d
2. b
3. d
4. a

page 65 Gray Whales, Amazing Travelers
1. c
2. d
3. b
4. a

page 66 Smart Stoplights
1. b
2. a
3. c
4. d

page 67 Reduce Your Carbon Footprint!
1. c
2. b
3. a
4. d

page 68 Disrupting Ecosystems
1. a
2. b
3. c
4. d

page 69 Robots
1. b
2. c
3. a
4. b

page 70 Deep-Sea Discoveries
1. b
2. a
3. c
4. d

Answer Key *(cont.)*

From the Past

page 73 Tasty Discoveries
1. c
2. a
3. b
4. d

page 74 From Trees to Ships
1. a
2. b
3. d
4. d

page 75 True Lighthouse Tales
1. b
2. a
3. d
4. c

page 76 Shipwrecked in Antarctica
1. a
2. b
3. a
4. c

page 77 The Discovery of Pompeii
1. b
2. c
3. a
4. c

page 78 World War II Submarines
1. d
2. b
3. c
4. d

page 79 Women Spies in the American Revolution
1. a
2. d
3. b
4. a

page 80 Surnames
1. b
2. c
3. a
4. d

page 81 Horses Helped Humans
1. b
2. a
3. d
4. c

page 82 Making Glass
1. d
2. a
3. d
4. c

page 83 A Whale of a Tale
1. d
2. b
3. a
4. c

page 84 The Dead Sea Scrolls
1. d
2. c
3. a
4. a

page 85 The Story of the Stars and Stripes
1. a
2. b
3. c
4. d

page 86 Mysterious Disappearances at Sea
1. d
2. b
3. d
4. a

page 87 Ancient Egyptian Mummies
1. a
2. c
3. b
4. c

page 88 Qin's Amazing Clay Army
1. b
2. c
3. a
4. d

page 89 Ghost Towns
1. d
2. d
3. a
4. c

page 90 The Story of the Statue of Liberty
1. a
2. c
3. b
4. d

page 91 The Legend of John Henry
1. b
2. c
3. b
4. a

page 92 Changing the World, One Page at a Time
1. a
2. b
3. b
4. c

page 93 Colossal Statues
1. b
2. a
3. c
4. d

page 94 Black Tuesday and the Great Depression
1. c
2. b
3. d
4. c

page 95 Curing Scurvy
1. b
2. a
3. b
4. d

page 96 The Story of the National Anthem
1. d
2. b
3. a
4. a

page 97 *The Jungle*: A Book That Shocked People
1. c
2. a
3. d
4. b

page 98 The Brownie Camera and the Photo Revolution
1. c
2. b
3. a
4. d

page 99 Lyuba, the Baby Woolly Mammoth
1. d
2. b
3. c
4. a

page 100 Dinosaur Discoveries
1. c
2. d
3. c
4. b

page 101 Animal Extinctions
1. d
2. d
3. b
4. a

page 102 Amazing Journeys on Foot
1. d
2. c
3. a
4. a

Did You Know?

page 105 All About Antelopes
1. b
2. c
3. c
4. d

Answer Key (cont.)

page 106 Was James Dean's Spider Jinxed?
1. b
2. d
3. a
4. d

page 107 Fleas
1. d
2. a
3. c
4. b

page 108 Worms Made Silk
1. a
2. b
3. d
4. a

page 109 Argan Oil
1. c
2. b
3. b
4. a

page 110 Ghost Lights Over Water
1. d
2. c
3. c
4. a

page 111 Chimpanzees Can Do Math!
1. c
2. d
3. a
4. c

page 112 Celebrity Shoplifter
1. d
2. c
3. d
4. b

page 113 A Museum Gets a Skeleton
1. c
2. b
3. a
4. d

page 114 Soap Nuts
1. d
2. c
3. b
4. a

page 115 Oil Rigs
1. b
2. d
3. d
4. a

page 116 Surviving Sailor
1. b
2. d
3. a
4. c

page 117 Missing Fortunes Underwater
1. a
2. d
3. c
4. b

page 118 The World's Longest-Burning Fire
1. a
2. b
3. c
4. a

page 119 Where Do Dead Satellites Go?
1. d
2. b
3. a
4. d

page 120 Newsflash: Prey Need Predators!
1. c
2. b
3. d
4. b

page 121 Sinkholes
1. d
2. b
3. c
4. a

page 122 Spider Legs Are Incredible
1. a
2. b
3. c
4. d

page 123 Amazing Saving Coincidences
1. c
2. b
3. a
4. d

page 124 The Janitor's Noisy Invention
1. d
2. a
3. d
4. c

page 125 When Booth Saved Lincoln's Life
1. d
2. b
3. a
4. c

page 126 Hot Dogs
1. a
2. c
3. b
4. a

page 127 Poisonous Plants
1. d
2. a
3. c
4. d

page 128 U.S. State Capitals' Names
1. b
2. c
3. d
4. c

page 129 Walruses
1. b
2. a
3. c
4. d

page 130 Fireworks
1. a
2. c
3. c
4. b

page 131 Speedy Cheetahs Are in Trouble
1. a
2. c
3. d
4. b

page 132 Skateboarding
1. d
2. b
3. c
4. b

page 133 An Unusual Relationship
1. d
2. a
3. b
4. c

page 134 Frozen Boy Survives
1. a
2. b
3. a
4. d

Fascinating People

page 137 Susan B. Anthony, Civil Rights Leader
1. b
2. c
3. a
4. a

Answer Key (cont.)

page 138 Dr. Seuss, Children's Author
1. a
2. d
3. b
4. c

page 139 Leif Ericson, Discoverer of North America
1. a
2. c
3. b
4. d

page 140 Barack Obama, 44th U.S. President
1. d
2. a
3. d
4. c

page 141 Oral Lee Brown, Philanthropist
1. b
2. c
3. c
4. a

page 142 Deborah Sampson, First U.S. Female Soldier
1. a
2. d
3. b
4. b

page 143 Jackie Robinson, Baseball Legend
1. a
2. b
3. c
4. d

page 144 The Fathers of Flight
1. b
2. d
3. a
4. c

page 145 Charles Shulz and the *Peanuts* Gang
1. b
2. d
3. b
4. c

page 146 Christopher Reeve, A Super Man
1. c
2. a
3. b
4. d

page 147 Sacagawea, Explorer
1. b
2. c
3. d
4. b

page 148 Dr. Edward Jenner, Smallpox Pioneer
1. c
2. b
3. d
4. a

page 149 Grandma Moses, Artist
1. a
2. d
3. d
4. c

page 150 Ida Lewis, Lime Rock Lighthouse Keeper
1. b
2. c
3. b
4. d

page 151 Crime-Fighting Granny
1. b
2. c
3. a
4. b

page 152 Louis Armstrong, Jazz Legend
1. c
2. b
3. a
4. c

page 153 Abraham Lincoln, 16th U.S. President
1. c
2. a
3. b
4. b

page 154 Walt Disney Changes Entertainment
1. d
2. a
3. c
4. c

page 155 Zhang Yin, Rich Recycler
1. c
2. a
3. c
4. b

page 156 Heroic Chiune Sugihara
1. c
2. a
3. b
4. a

page 157 Harry Houdini, Master Magician
1. d
2. a
3. b
4. c

page 158 Dat So La Lee, Basket Weaver
1. b
2. c
3. a
4. b

page 159 Joe Loius, the Brown Bomber
1. a
2. d
3. c
4. a

page 160 Supermex, the Pro Golfer
1. b
2. a
3. c
4. d

page 161 The Female Moses
1. c
2. d
3. b
4. d

page 162 Brave Irena Sendler
1. a
2. d
3. c
4. b

page 163 Golda Meir, Israel's Heroine
1. b
2. a
3. c
4. b

page 164 Franklin Chang-Díaz, Astronaut and Physicist
1. a
2. d
3. b
4. c

page 165 The Tale of Beatrix Potter
1. c
2. b
3. a
4. d

page 166 Fannie Farmer Changes Cooking
1. b
2. d
3. b
4. a

Leveling Chart

Page #	Flesch-Kincaid Grade Level	Page #	Flesch-Kincaid Grade Level	Page #	Flesch-Kincaid Grade Level
Interesting Places and Events		**Scientifically Speaking** (cont.)		**Did You Know?** (cont.)	
9	3.2	62	3.6	116	3.9
10	3.0	63	3.5	117	3.3
11	3.2	64	3.9	118	3.5
12	4.6*	65	4.2*	119	3.9
13	3.3	66	3.7	120	3.5
14	3.0	67	4.4*	121	4.1*
15	3.3	68	4.0	122	3.5
16	3.2	69	3.9	123	3.5
17	3.2	70	3.8	124	3.7
18	3.4	**From the Past**		125	3.6
19	3.3	73	3.0	126	3.9
20	3.5	74	3.2	127	3.8
21	3.3	75	3.2	128	6.3*
22	3.5	76	3.2	129	3.7
23	3.5	77	3.2	130	4.0
24	3.6	78	3.5	131	3.8
25	3.5	79	3.4	132	4.0
26	3.8	80	3.4	133	3.6
27	3.7	81	3.4	134	3.7
28	3.6	82	3.6	**Fascinating People**	
29	4.0	83	3.4	137	3.4
30	3.6	84	3.3	138	3.2
31	3.8	85	3.4	139	4.0
32	4.0	86	3.5	140	4.5*
33	3.8	87	3.5	141	3.1
34	3.9	88	3.5	142	3.3
35	3.9	89	3.7	143	3.7
36	4.3*	90	4.0	144	3.2
37	3.9	91	3.6	145	4.1*
38	3.8	92	3.5	146	3.5
Scientifically Speaking		93	3.9	147	5.4*
41	3.2	94	3.8	148	3.5
42	3.0	95	3.8	149	3.4
43	3.0	96	4.0	150	3.6
44	3.0	97	3.8	151	3.8
45	3.0	98	3.8	152	3.6
46	3.1	99	3.8	153	3.5
47	3.2	100	3.8	154	3.6
48	3.3	101	4.3*	155	4.3*
49	3.3	102	3.9	156	4.8*
50	3.2	**Did You Know?**		157	3.6
51	3.3	105	3.1	158	3.8
52	3.2	106	3.0	159	3.9
53	3.3	107	3.2	160	3.6
54	3.3	108	3.1	161	3.6
55	3.4	109	3.1	162	3.8
56	3.4	110	3.3	163	3.7
57	3.6	111	3.1	164	3.8
58	4.0	112	3.5	165	3.8
59	3.5	113	3.4	166	3.9
60	3.7	114	3.1		
61	3.9	115	3.4		

Tracking Sheet

Interesting Places and Events		Scientifically Speaking		From the Past		Did You Know?		Fascinating People	
Page 9		Page 41		Page 73		Page 105		Page 137	
Page 10		Page 42		Page 74		Page 106		Page 138	
Page 11		Page 43		Page 75		Page 107		Page 139	
Page 12		Page 44		Page 76		Page 108		Page 140	
Page 13		Page 45		Page 77		Page 109		Page 141	
Page 14		Page 46		Page 78		Page 110		Page 142	
Page 15		Page 47		Page 79		Page 111		Page 143	
Page 16		Page 48		Page 80		Page 112		Page 144	
Page 17		Page 49		Page 81		Page 113		Page 145	
Page 18		Page 50		Page 82		Page 114		Page 146	
Page 19		Page 51		Page 83		Page 115		Page 147	
Page 20		Page 52		Page 84		Page 116		Page 148	
Page 21		Page 53		Page 85		Page 117		Page 149	
Page 22		Page 54		Page 86		Page 118		Page 150	
Page 23		Page 55		Page 87		Page 119		Page 151	
Page 24		Page 56		Page 88		Page 120		Page 152	
Page 25		Page 57		Page 89		Page 121		Page 153	
Page 26		Page 58		Page 90		Page 122		Page 154	
Page 27		Page 59		Page 91		Page 123		Page 155	
Page 28		Page 60		Page 92		Page 124		Page 156	
Page 29		Page 61		Page 93		Page 125		Page 157	
Page 30		Page 62		Page 94		Page 126		Page 158	
Page 31		Page 63		Page 95		Page 127		Page 159	
Page 32		Page 64		Page 96		Page 128		Page 160	
Page 33		Page 65		Page 97		Page 129		Page 161	
Page 34		Page 66		Page 98		Page 130		Page 162	
Page 35		Page 67		Page 99		Page 131		Page 163	
Page 36		Page 68		Page 100		Page 132		Page 164	
Page 37		Page 69		Page 101		Page 133		Page 165	
Page 38		Page 70		Page 102		Page 134		Page 166	

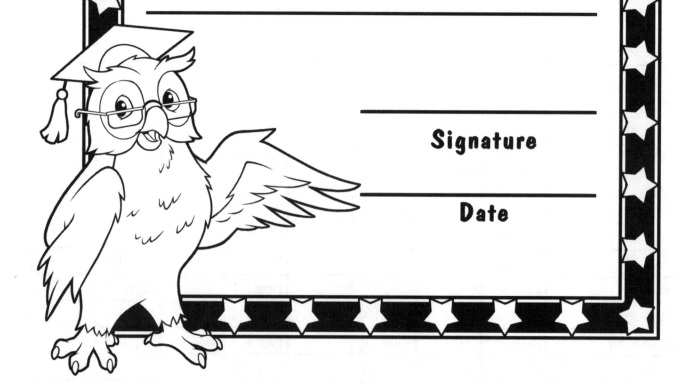

Congratulations

to

_____

for completing

_____

_____

_____
Signature

_____
Date